APQ LIBRARY OF
PHILOSOPHY

APQ LIBRARY OF PHILOSOPHY
Nicholas Rescher, Editor

THE PHILOSOPHY OF CHARLES S. PEIRCE
A Critical Introduction
ROBERT ALMEDER

TWO CENTURIES OF PHILOSOPHY
American Philosophy Since the Revolution
PETER CAWS (ed.)

RATIONAL BELIEF SYSTEMS
BRIAN ELLIS

THE NATURE OF PHILOSOPHY
JOHN KEKES

INTRODUCTION TO THE
PHILOSOPHY OF MATHEMATICS
HUGH LEHMAN

VALUE AND EXISTENCE
JOHN LESLIE

RECENT WORK IN PHILOSOPHY
KENNETH G. LACEY and TIBOR R. MACHAN (eds.)

PLATO ON BEAUTY, WISDOM,
AND THE ARTS
JULIUS MORAVCSIK and PHILIP TEMKO (eds.)

KNOWLEDGE AND SCEPTICISM
DOUGLAS ODEGARD

LEIBNIZ:
An Introduction to His Philosophy
NICHOLAS RESCHER

THE LOGIC OF INCONSISTENCY
A Study in Nonstandard Possible-World
Semantics and Ontology
NICHOLAS RESCHER and ROBERT BRANDOM

THE NATURE
OF
KNOWLEDGE

ALAN R. WHITE

ROWMAN AND LITTLEFIELD
Totowa, New Jersey

First published in the United States 1982 by Rowman and Littlefield,
81 Adams Drive, Totowa, New Jersey 07512.

Distributed in the U.K. and Commonwealth by
George Prior Associated Publishers Limited
High Holborn House
53154 High Holborn
London WC1 V 6RL
England

Library of Congress Cataloging in Publication Data

White, Alan R.
  The nature of knowledge.

  (APQ library of philosophy)
  Bibliography: p.
  Includes index.
  1. Knowledge, Theory of.   I. Title.   II. Series.
BD161.W43 1982   121   81-23450
ISBN 0-8476-7073-2   AACR2

Printed in the United States of America

Contents

Acknowledgments

I am grateful to the editors of *Mind, Analysis,* the *Canadian Journal of Philosophy* and the *Proceedings of the Aristotelian Society* for permission to use material which originally appeared in their journals.

CHAPTER I

Knowledge and Claims to Knowledge

Much philosophical investigation of the nature of knowledge commonly begins by assimilating it to, and confusing it with, an investigation of claims to knowledge. Thus, one recent book begins "Questions such as 'What can be known?' and 'How do we know what we know?'—questions about what claims to knowledge can in principle be justified, and how they can be justified—are. . . ."[1] Another moves so whole-heartedly, yet almost unconsciously, from the declared aim of "formulating necessary and sufficient conditions for a man's having knowledge" to the aim of "explaining how knowledge claims may be justified" that it devotes more than two-thirds of its space to the notion of justification.[2] A third recent investigation of knowledge emerges as a formal logic of statements of knowledge, whose status partly depends on who makes them.[3] Even an author who explicitly declares that his task "is not that of investigating knowledge *per se* but merely that of investigating epistemic justification" assumes that the "task of the epistemologist is to explain how it is possible for us to know that P, *i.e.*, to explain what justifies us in believing the things we do".[4] This shift has spread to investigations of memory; a recent work says "People do remember things; but that is just to say that they can and do make memory claims."[5]

   Such an assimilation is understandable, since philosophers commonly approach the world, not directly, but *via* people's statements about the world. They first narrow their enquiry whether someone knows something to the enquiry whether the statement that he knows it is true. They then narrow this latter, first, to the enquiry whether *his* statement that he knows it is true and then to a many-sided enquiry into his statement, including the question whether his statement is justified and whether he is justified in

1

making it.[6] Since his statement that he knows something would be expressed in the first person present indicative as "I know so-and-so," the final shift in philosophical enquiry is to an examination of this form of words.[7] The difference between an enquiry whether someone knows something and an enquiry whether the statement or claim that he knows it is *true* or valid need not be great. Nor need there be much difference between the latter and an enquiry whether *his* statement that he knows it or his claim to know it is *true*. But a big, though often unnoticed, step is taken from the latter to an enquiry into the *justification* of his claim to know it and an even bigger step to an enquiry into the justification of his belief either in it or in his knowledge of it. I shall suggest that some questions which are appropriate about someone's claim to know something are not necessarily appropriate about the nature of what it is to know something and that the assimilation of these two enquiries has caused confusion.

Now, clearly, not every use of "I know so-and-so" is to *claim* knowledge. This form of words may be used for a multitude of purposes, e.g., to report one's knowledge, to admit, confess or concede it or to acknowledge, reveal or assert it. It may also be used to express one's confidence, to assure one's audience, to accept someone's statement or to guarantee one's story.[8] But using it to claim that one knows is a common use; and I shall, henceforth, merely for convenience, often talk of a "claim to knowledge" for anyone's assertion of knowledge as contrasted with his possession of it.

There are further reasons for the philosopher's shift in interest from the possession of knowledge to claims to knowledge other than his preference for statements over what statements are about. First, everyday investigations of the possession of knowledge often arise as the result of claims made, e.g., by examination candidates, by student classes, by witnesses, informers, newspaper reporters, historians, scientists or whatever. Secondly, much of what we know we either know, or at least think, that we know and are, therefore, willing and ready to say that we know it. Thirdly, philosophers often consider their job to be that of examining, and perhaps refuting, the sceptical query whether and how we know all that we commonly or unreflectively *think* and *claim* we know. Further, in order to do this they lay out explicitly and fully for investigation the reasons and arguments that could be or have been given for thus *holding* that such and such a kind of thing can be and is known. Fourthly, philosophers have, as we shall see, traditionally since Plato approached the notion of knowledge *via* the notion of belief, asking what has to be added to belief to make it an instance of knowledge. But, since a person who believes something will, even more than a person who knows something, normally be aware of this and willing to express his belief, we are usually presented with a situation where our problem is to differentiate between someone who is willing only to express a belief in so and so and someone who is willing to claim that he does not merely believe it, but knows it. Finally, philosophers[9] have, under the influence of J. L. Austin,[10] recently turned their interest from what one *says* to what one *does* when one says it, from what it is to know something to what it is to say that one knows something, e.g., to make a claim, to guarantee one's story or to assure one's audience.

There is, of course, a legitimate connection between an enquiry into the nature of knowledge and one into claims to knowledge in that the criteria for any valid or justified claim depend on what it is a claim to, whether knowledge or something else. But a connection is not an identity.

The point of emphasising the slide from an investigation into the nature of knowledge to an investigation into claims to knowledge is that it has had several effects on philosophical analyses of knowledge, that is, on philosophical answers to the question "What is knowledge?." We shall see, for instance, that two of the three traditional philosophical criteria of knowledge, namely the presence of a belief, or even of a feeling of certainty, in the existence or the correctness of what is known and the justification of, or the right to, such a belief, or feeling of certainty, borrow much of their plausibility as criteria from their appropriateness to the assessment of someone's claims to knowledge.[11] For example, the question whether one is sure that the Tropic of Cancer is north of the Tropic of Capricorn and what justification one has for being sure of this may be more relevant to an investigation of someone's assertion that he knows this than to the question whether he does know it and to the question what it is to know it. This is why to say sincerely "I know so and so, but I'm not certain of it" is strange, even though it is quite common for us not to be certain of many things we know. This is not, however, to say either that someone who is unsure of something won't claim to know it or that, if he does not claim to know it, he must be unsure of it. There can be various reasons for claiming or not claiming. Equally, it is not to say that someone who does not claim because he is unsure would not be justified in claiming, since his reasons for being unsure may be bad ones or be reasons which are outweighed by other good ones. Somewhat similarly, the thesis, held by many philosophers, that someone who knows something must think that he does know it is different from, and I shall later argue less plausible than, the thesis that someone who claims or sincerely asserts that he knows it must think that he does. If one supposes that a man who knows the date of Leibniz's birth must think that it was 1646 or supposes that he must think that he knows the date, it is reasonable to side with the common philosophical demand that such a man should be able to give some reason for thinking either of these and be able to give some evidence for what he thinks he knows. Hence, the recent popularity of enquiries into the justification of claims to knowledge.[12] But anyone who allows that a man may know something without thinking that he does so will not feel the same need to argue that the possession of knowledge requires of its possessor any ability to give reasons for his possession of it or to give evidence for what he possesses, even though there is a reason why he should possess it and there is evidence for what he possesses.

Furthermore, the thesis[13] that one can always discover by reflection and, hence, know whether one knows something or only believes it would also be more plausible if what reflection was alleged to discover was the difference between believing something and claiming to know it and not the difference between believing something and actually knowing it. For the second difference depends on factors outside one's control in a way that the first need not. The first enquiry is whether or not we are doing something, that is claiming to know, while the second is whether or not we are in possession of something. Similarly, reflection might be able to tell me whether I am using the words "I know" in a particular way, but not whether or not I know in some way.[14]

Again, the paradoxical nature of the non-contradictory assertion that I know that p but I'm not certain that p has led some to
suppose that there must be a "conceptual link between knowledge
and certainty".[15] But this no more follows than that the paradoxical
nature of "I believe that to-morrow is Tuesday, but it isn't" shows
a conceptual link between belief and existence or truth. Finally,
philosophers who confine their attention to "I know" sometimes[16]
move illegitimately from the thesis that "I know" has many of
what Austin called "illocutionary uses", e.g., to claim, admit,
concede, confess to knowledge or express certainty, to the thesis
that "know" has many senses, one corresponding to each illocutionary use. They confuse what "know" is used to do with what it
is used to say. Furthermore, they sometimes conclude that because some of the conditions arguably necessary for the appropriateness of saying "I know" are absent, therefore, this is not an
example of something one does at the time know. Thus, it is argued
that because it is inappropriate to tell an audience something so
obvious as that one knows one is standing in front of them, therefore that one is standing in front of them is not a good example of
something one knows.

Whether or not the frequent assimilation of enquiries into the
nature and possession of knowledge to enquiries into the assertion
of or claim to knowledge is the cause of false theses about knowledge, there can be no doubt that such an assimilation is a mistake.
What one claims is quite different from one's claim to it and an
investigation of the former quite different from an investigation of
the latter.

Clearly, the assertion that someone, whether one-self or another, knows something does not guarantee that one knows it. We
frequently say of another or claim for ourselves that we know what
in fact we do not know. Conversely, there are lots of things one
knows that one never claims to know or that no one else ever
asserts that one knows, however true such a claim or assertion
would be if it were made.

There are many factors relevant to a claim to knowledge which
are not relevant to knowledge or its possession. To claim to know
or to assert that one knows is to do something, namely to say
something, whereas to know something is obviously not to say

anything and we shall see that it is not to do anything either. Hence, we can repeat our claim to knowledge, but not repeat our knowing. We can tend to claim to know something, but not tend to know it. To cease to claim is not to cease to know, nor is to cease to know to cease to claim. Claims to knowledge, but not knowledge or its possession, can be stupid, obstinate, passionate and groundless or sensible, hesitant, sincere and well supported. We can willingly, reluctantly or deliberately claim to know, as we can in these ways promise, warn or deny, but not willingly, reluctantly or deliberately know. We can ask someone to, or wish that he would not, promise, warn, deny or claim to know, but not ask him or wish that he would not know. We can ask what moves a person to say he knows, but not what moves him to know. We have already seen that in addition to asking whether a claim to knowledge is valid or not, we can also ask whether one is justified in making it and can, therefore, ask what would justify it. But no question arises of justifying our knowledge itself as contrasted with showing, in answer to the sceptic, how it is possible to have it. This is why we can ask why one claims or asserts that one knows so and so, but not why one knows it and, on the other hand, how one knows it, but not, in this sense, how one claims or asserts this. The question "How does he (you, we) know so and so?" is different from the question "How could he (you, we) show that he (you, we) knows so and so?" even though some of what answers the one may answer the other.

We have also seen that a question about the confidence or certainty with which one claims or asserts that one knows something is different from a question about any confidence or certainty one has in what one knows. One can claim or assert with confidence or certainty, but not know with confidence or certainty. Claiming with certainty to know is not knowing for certain. Furthermore, the legitimate difference between the validity of a claim to knowedge, that is the truth of the assertion that one knows, and the justifiability of making that claim, whether or not it is true, has no parallel with knowledge itself. Either one knows or one does not. Thus, while we can say that, e.g., people in the fifteenth century were justified on their evidence in claiming that they knew that the earth was flat, though their claim was false, we can only say that they did not know that the earth was flat. Unfortunately, the distinction between the criteria for appropriately saying one knows and for the truth of what one says is sometimes blurred[17] because "being right to say so and so" and "being right in saying so and so" are both put as "rightly saying so and so". So that the fact that one who has good reason for saying that he knows so and so even when, unknown to himself, he does not know it can be said to have rightly said that he knew it is thought to be evidence for the view that he was right in saying that he knew something which he did not know. It is simply a mistake to argue[18] that because what one does when one says "I know" may sometimes be the same as what one does when one says "I'm sure", e.g., express one's confidence, therefore what I say when I say the former may sometimes be the same as what I say when I say the latter and, hence, that the two are synonymous. Clearly, disproving one of these is not disproving the other.

What, therefore, I am going to enquire into is the nature of knowledge and its possession and not the justification of a claim to possess it. I make no assumption about which enquiry is the more important.

CHAPTER 2

Objects of Knowledge

A. INTRODUCTION

In the *Theaetetus* Socrates chided a fellow symposiast for attempting to answer the question "What is knowledge?" by simply giving examples of the things which we know, e.g., geometry, carpentry and the art of cobbling. And certainly one must distinguish between what it is to know something and what is or can be known. Yet, just as a scientist takes care not to jump to conclusions from a narrow set of data, so a philosopher must beware of taking a distorted view because of a one-sided diet of examples. Too many philosophical analyses of knowledge, including Plato's, have been restricted to a particular kind of thing that can be known, especially the kind that is expressed in English as "knowing that p", e.g., that 1815 is the date of the Battle of Waterloo or that there is no life after death. Hence, it is important to remind ourselves of the wide range of things which it makes sense to say, whether truly or falsely, that we know.

(1) The verb "know" can be followed by an interrogative such as whether what, who, where, when, which, why or how, with a verb either (a) in the indicative or (b) in the infinitive, as when one knows who did it or whom to ask, what happened or what to do, how it fell or how to jump.

(2) "Know" can occasionally be followed by the relative "what", as when one already knows what one is being told.

(3) The various ways in which "know" can be followed by a noun or noun-phrase include (a) that in which the noun-phrase is a variation on an interrogative, as when one knows the colour, weight or size of the curtains, the date, location, cause or result of the battle or the heavyweight champion of the world. For to know any of these is to know what or who it is; (b) that in which the noun indicates something we can learn and know how to speak, recite or calculate, as when we know French, the Ballad of Reading Gaol or one's mathematical tables; (c) that in which the noun indicates a

person, place, condition or thing of which one acquires knowledge by acquaintance or direct experience, as when one knows one's neighbours, the heavyweight champion of the world, the town in which one lives, or has been lucky never to have known poverty, pain or hunger, or such inflation, stupidity or class-hatred as is current today.

(4) "Know" is frequently followed by an infinitive clause as when one knows a man to be honest, a gear box to be faulty or a statement to be true.

(5) Finally, and frequently, "know" is followed by a that-nominalisation, as when one knows that the battle was lost, that it is raining, that there will be no more supplies this week or that something should, must or ought to be done or happen.

When we look at these linguistic variations in more detail, we shall see, I think, that, first, they can be reduced to three broad conceptual classes, namely, (a) "know" followed by an interrogative, whether explicitly, as in "knowing where or how A V's or where or how to V," or implicitly, as in "knowing the colour, weight or size of something" or "knowing French or one's twelve times table;" (b) "knowing that," as in "knowing that the sun is larger than the moon" and (c) knowing by acquaintance, as in "knowing one's next door neighbours or the environs of Paris." Secondly, the first two classes can be shown to be basically the same, namely "knowing that." They differ only in that the first states what it is to which one knows the answer, while the second states the answer which one knows. Thirdly, the objects of the third class can be shown not to be "objects of knowledge" in the same sense in which the objects of the other two classes are. They do not give an answer to the question "What do we know?." Hence, my general conclusions will be that what it is to know something is the same whatever we know and that what we know is of the same kind however it is expressed.

B. "KNOW" WITH AN INTERROGATIVE, I.E., WHETHER, WHAT, WHO, WHEN, WHERE, WHICH, HOW AND WHY.

The verb "know" can be followed by an interrogative, that is, as grammarians sometimes say, can take a wh-nominalisation. And this in two different ways, namely an interrogative with a verb in the indicative and an interrogative with a verb in the infinitive. Thus, one can know what, whom, where, when or how A V's, e.g., where the treasure is, what is said in the Book of Genesis or how the subjunctive is used in Greek, and one can know what, whom, where or how *to* V, e.g., where to go, what to do, whom to ask or how to swim.

(i) . . . . . . A V's

"Know" followed by an interrogative and a verb in the indicative mood is a variety of "know that." Thus, to know what, whom, where, when or how A V's is to know the thing, person, place, time or way A V's, or, in other words, to know what is the thing, person, place, time or way A V's.[1] And this is to know *that* so and so is the thing, person, place, time or way which A V's.[2] For example, to know where A buried the treasure or to know the place in which he buried it is to know that A buried the treasure in such and such an unmentioned place; and to know when he buried it or the time at which he buried it is to know that he buried it at such and such an unmentioned time; and to know how he buried it or to know the way he buried it is to know that he buried it in such and such an unmentioned way. Similarly, learning, discovering, forgetting, showing, telling or being taught what, whom, where, when or how A V's or learning, discovering, forgetting, etc., the thing, person, place, time or way A V's is learning, discovering, forgetting, etc., that such and such is the thing, person, place, time or way in which A V's.

(ii) . . . . . TO V

About "know" followed by an interrogative and a verb in the infinitive mood, that is, to know what, whom, where, when or how to V, two questions immediately arise. Are there any important conceptual differences *either* (a) between "know" followed by an interrogative and infinitive and "know" followed by an interrogative and indicative *or* (b) between "know" followed by most interrogatives, either with the indicative or the infinitive, and "know" followed by the interrogative "how" and the infinitive, as in "knowing how to swim" and "knowing how to find?" The answer to both questions I shall now proceed to argue is "No."

(a) "Know" followed by an interrogative and infinitive has an analysis parallel to that of "know" followed by an interrogative and indicative. Hence, to know what, whom, where, when or how *to* V is to know the thing, person, place, time or way to V or, in other words, to know what is the thing, person, place, time or way to V. And to know this is to know *that* such and such is the thing, person, place, time or way to V. Thus, to know what to charge for the book, whom to ask, where to look for a spanner, when to arrive or how to address an Archbishop or to save petrol is to know that so and so is the price to charge for the book, the place to look for a spanner, the time to arrive, the person to ask, or the way to address an Archbishop or to save petrol.

So much is sufficient to show that knowing what, whom, where, when or how *to* V is as clearly a case of knowing *that* as is knowing what, whom, where, when or how A V's.[3] Though, therefore, it is not necessary to investigate the exact differences between the indicative construction, e.g., to know when or how, that is, the place or way, A V's, and the infinitive construction, e.g., to know where or how, that is, the place or way, to V, such an investigation may throw some further light on the meaning of "knowing where or how to V."

"Know" followed by an interrogative and infinitive seems to be a grammatical variation on "know" followed by an interrogative and a modal verb. The choice of modal seems to depend on whether the verb in the infinitive is a "task" or "achievement" verb.

(a) 1. One should V

First, when the interrogative is followed—as any interrogative can be—by the infinitive of a "task" verb, the modal seems to be "should." Thus, to know whom to ask is to whom one should ask, to know what to call one's dog is to know what one should call one's dog, to know where to look for a spanner is to know where one should look, to know when to turn on the tap is to know when one should turn it on. So, to know how to address an Archbishop is to know how one should address him and to know how to reason, to conduct enquiries, to behave at funerals, to cook aubergines, to fish, to play chess or the guitar, is to know how one should do these various things. Such an equivalence between the infinitive construction and the construction with the modal "should" occurs with many words. Thus, if it is only fair, proper, reasonable, traditional, for women to go first, it is only fair, proper, reasonable, traditional that women should go first; if my age is a reason for me to take things easy, it is a reason why I should take things easy. To advise or persuade someone to V is to advise or persuade him that he should V; to intend to be the first there or to intend someone to suffer is to intend that one should be the first there or that he should suffer.

2. *One can V*

When, however, the interrogative is followed—as some, but not all, can be—by the infinitive of an "achievement" verb, the modal seems to be "can." Thus, to know where to find a spanner is to know where one can find it and to know how to discover gold, to detect misprints, to win arguments, to persuade juries, to get to the station, to save petrol, to hold one's breath under water, to contact the police in case of emergency or to tell the date of a piece of silver from its hall-mark is to know how one can do any of these.

If "know" with an interrogative and infinitive can be interpreted as "know" with an interrogative and a modal, one can relate "knowing" what, whom, where, when or how *to* V to "knowing what, whom, where, when or how A V's as "knowing what, whom, where, when or how A *should* or *can* V" to "knowing what, whom, where, when or how A V's." Equally one can learn, discover, forget, be unable to think or recall, be sure, tell or teach what, whom, where, when or how to V—or, what is the same, what, whom, where, when or how one should (or can) V—and what, whom, where, when or how A does V. I can learn or forget, be informed or shown, how to get to the bus station, where to park my car or when to stop singing as I can learn or forget, be informed or shown, how a bus works, where the car park is or when the singing stops. But "knowing where or how one should (can) V" as a variant on "knowing where or how to V" is more restricted than "knowing where or how one does V." Thus, the former is confined to verbs of action, attainment and, perhaps, attitude, e.g., where to look or find, how to shoot or score, when to go or arrive, whom to blame or believe, what to ask or expect; whereas the latter takes any kind of verb, e.g., how he did it, when it happened, where it was found, when it will be, whom it affects, why he feels so, etc. In the former, the subject of the modal clause must be either the impersonal "one" or the same as the subject of the main clause. Thus, to know what to do, where to find something, whom to believe, or how to get to the station is to know what I or one should do, where I or one can find it, whom I or one should believe or how I or one can get to the station. In the latter, the subjects of the main and subsidiary verbs are quite independent. I may know how you feel, you may know what he feels, and he may know where it happened.

Knowing what, where, when, whom or how A does V is, as we saw, knowing *that* A does V an unspecified thing or person in an unspecified place, at an unspecified time, in an unspecified way. For example, to know where A buried the treasure is to know that he buried it at a place not mentioned and to know how he solved the problem is to know that he solved it in a way of which we are not informed. Similarly, knowing what, where, when, whom or how one should (or can) V is knowing *that* one should (or can) V an unspecified person or thing in an unspecified place, time and way. For example, to know where to get cheap petrol is to know that one can get it at an unmentioned place and to know how to address an Archbishop is to know that one should address him in a way of which we are not told.

(b) How to V

Some thirty years ago Gilbert Ryle attempted to show, first in his Presidential Address to the Aristotelian Society in 1945[4] and later in his *Concept of Mind,*[5] that *knowing how to* do something, e.g., to play chess or the cello, to ride a bicycle or to talk grammatically, is not only essentially different from *knowing that* something is so, e.g., that there was a Roman ford across the Humber or that the

German word for knife is "Messer," but is equivalent to *being able to* do that which one knows how to do. I shall argue that both of Ryle's theses are mistaken.

To take Ryle's second thesis first, namely, that to know how to do something is to be able to do it;[6] it is clear that neither in fact implies the other. It is possible, and indeed quite common, to know how to do something without being able to do it and even more common to be able to do something without knowing how to do it. And this lack of any logical connection exists whether what one is able to or knows how to do is something of a certain sort, such as playing chess, swimming or cooking, which will, therefore, involve a general ability or knowledge, or a specific instance, such as spelling a particular word, opening a particular window or getting into contact with a particular colleague, which does not involve any general ability or kind of knowledge. It also exists whether what one knows how to do is a task or an achievement.

That to be able to do something does not imply knowing how to do it is most obvious in those cases where the former notion is applicable, but the latter is not. This may be either because knowledge is not relevant to the type of ability or because it is not relevant to the type of possessor of that ability or because it is not relevant to the type of activity or achievement for which there is an ability.

First, if X does V, there is at least a weak sense in which it follows that it "can" or "is able to" V—the implication which mediaevalists called "ab esse ad posse"—but not necessarily that it "knows how to" V. A plant which grows in the shade shows that it is able to do so, but clearly not that it knows how to. If I actually feel the heat of the fire from here, I "can" feel it, though I don't know how to feel it.

Secondly, only animate, indeed intelligent, creatures can possess a knowledge of how to do something; but the inanimate have abilities, often indeed the same abilities, as much as the animate. Ships are as able to float as sailors, fish as able to breathe under water as frogmen, machines as able to calculate or to play chess as men and the sundew flower as able to catch its prey as any human predator; but only men and animals can acquire or possess the knowledge of how to do these things.

Thirdly, there are a host of activities and achievements, usually of a physical kind, the ability to do which, whether innate or acquired, is unrelated, even in human beings, to any knowledge. Thus, my ability to hear traffic or to see across the room, to hold about five pints of beer or to do without sleep for about 18 hours does not imply and is not due to any knowledge of mine any more than my inability to hear sounds which my dog can hear, to see as far as those of you who have no need of spectacles, to drink as much as some of my colleagues or to do with as little sleep as others is due to some lack of knowledge. These are not things I normally discover, find out or learn how to do, in which I am trained or become practised, which I remember or forget, or which I am myself taught or teach others.

These very examples, in fact, give a clue to the causal, not logical, relation between the ability to do something and the knowledge of how to do it. It is because knowledge is logically alien to the inanimate and unnecessary for the physiological that neither the machine's ability to beat me at chess nor your ability to see further than I can implies any know-how on its or your part.[7] These abilities have other causes. This is why the exception here proves the rule. For, though increasing years bring with them longer sight and less need of sleep, I can also improve my physiological abilities by acquiring some knowledge. I can increase my long distance sight by using the knowledge that narrowing the pupil concentrates the entrance of light rays, I can increase my ability to go without sleep by using my knowledge of stimulants and I may lengthen my life because of what I read in an article on how to live longer. Conversely, it may be that some abilities, such as the ability to play chess or the cello, to detect misprints or fallacies, to tie reef knots or to make good jokes are normally only acquirable by using one's knowledge. Thus, children are, perhaps, born able to blink but have to learn how to wink and most of us have to acquire and use knowledge before we are able to play chess or spot fallacies. I may be unable to secure the boat because I have forgotten how to tie a bowline or unable to solve your problem because I've forgotten how to extract square roots. My inability to get hold of a colleague on holiday is due to my not knowing how to get a message to someone who is not available by the usual means of 'phone, post, radio, etc. But even here the existence of machines which can play chess or detect misprints and fallacies, and the logical possibility that we could have been born able to wink and to see jokes show that here also the connection of being able to V and knowing how to V is causal, not logical.

But, not only does being able to do something not either logically or physically entail knowing how to do it, knowing how to do it does not logically or physically entail being able to do it. Though it may be that whatever a subject—and, of course, here the subject is necessarily an intelligent creature—knows how to do is something of which it at least makes sense to say that he is able to do it, it need not be true that he is able to do it. For, there are all sorts of things which can make me unable to do what I know very well how to do. I may know how to open a tin which I have not the strength to open myself, or to save money which weakness of will makes me unable to do. What deprives me, whether temporarily or permanently, of an ability which I once had need not make me forget, either for the moment or for all time, what I once knew. The lack of means and materials, the accidents of time and place, the presence of hindrances and restraints, which temporarily make me unable, e.g., to move my arm, to make my escape, to carry out an experiment, to tie this knot, do not make me forget how to do it or temporarily banish the knowledge from my mind. Nor does the permanent injury which cripples a driver, the paralysis which ends a swimmer's career or the arthritis which numbs the seamstress's fingers, deprive them of the knowledge of how to drive, to swim or to sew, in the way that a head injury or disease of the brain might do. This is not to argue, wrongly,[8] that each momentary hindrance of the exercise of an ability or every lack of opportunity to exercise it implies the loss of that ability or to suppose that each moment of forgetfulness implies a loss of knowledge or of memory. I don't lose my ability to ride a bicycle because there is no bicycle handy on which I could display the ability nor do I cease to know how to play chess because I have no chess set by me. But there are cases where an ability is lost and not merely hindered in or lacking opportunity for its manifestation. What is being argued is that there is no necessary concomitance between the loss of an ability to V, temporary or permanent, and the loss of the knowledge how to V; and that the varied causes of the one are not necessarily causes of the other. That this has been overlooked may be due to the fact that the purely intellectual abilities characteristic of human beings, such as the ability to speak and to argue, to play chess and to joke, may have knowledge as their only causes—though the increased sophistication of machines throws this in doubt—and that, therefore, there is no way in which the ability could be lost without a loss in the knowledge. Expert drivers, swimmers and seamstresses can pass on to us their knowledge of how to do what they themselves can no longer do, but what could a grammarian tell us who could no longer parse or a wit who had lost the ability to see a joke?

The truth is that there are some, perhaps few, abilities for which knowing how is a causally necessary condition and many for which it is not, while other abilities which do not normally require such knowledge can be acquired through it. Conversely, there are abilities for which knowing how is a causally sufficient condition and others for which it is not. But whereas knowing how to do something may make me able to do it, it makes no sense to say that being able to do something can give me a knowledge of how to do it. Likewise, inability to recognise an oboe, a Boeing 747 or a piece of bad philosophy can be the effect, but not the cause, of my ignorance.

It has been alleged by D. G. Brown[9] that, though in what he calls the "standard use" knowing how to do something admittedly neither implies nor is implied by being able to do it, there is a second use of the phrase "know how to do" so and so—dubbed by Brown the "English use"—which does express something which is implied by being able to do it and that, therefore, contrapositively, not knowing how to do so and so does, in this use, imply being unable to do it. Thus, to take his own examples, though he wants to allow that not knowing how to move about in a boat or to address a magistrate does not imply being unable to do these things—and presumably he would admit that not knowing how to hold six pints of liquid or to breathe does not make one unable to do these—he argues that not knowing how to run a projector or to build frame houses does imply an inability to do these.

But, first, the examples contain an important hidden difference

which has nothing to do with the meaning of "know how to" but
with the meaning of the words used to express the examples. Thus,
Brown has really shifted from "not knowing how to move about in
a boat correctly", e.g., so as not to upset it, or "not knowing how
to address a magistrate correctly," e.g., by the conventional title
reserved for magistrates as contrasted with High Court Judges and
Lords of Appeal, to "being unable to move about in a boat at all"
or "being unable to speak to a magistrate in any way." For it is, as
Brown admits, just as plausible that an accused who does not know
how to address a magistrate correctly is unable to bring out the
correct address as that a man who does not know how to run a
projector—presumably in such a way that the slides are shown as
they should be—will be unable to do so. It is, however, equally
plausible, on the other hand—as Brown seems grudgingly to admit
on pp. 241–2—that a man who does not know how to build a house
or run a projector correctly will be able to put up some sort of
house or get some results from a projector as that a man who does
not know how to move about in a boat (correctly) or to address a
magistrate (correctly) is able to do some moving about in the boat
or say something to the magistrate.

Attempts to show[10] or assertions[11] that one Greek word for
"knowledge", namely "ἐπιστήμη" (and its corresponding verb),
sometimes means "know how" and implies or is synonymous with
"ability" (δύναμις) or "skill" (τέχνη) really prove no more than
that the verb plus the infinitive, like "savoir" and the infinitive,
means "know how to" and that there are some things which we
can both know how to do, be able to do and be skilled at doing.

The difference between the examples in which there seems to be
a connection between the ability to do something and the knowledge how to do it and those in which there seems to be no connection is that in the former set "knowing how to V" is knowing how
one can V, but in the latter it is knowing how one should V. This is
why examples of the former set usually contain "achievement"
verbs and examples of the latter contain "task" verbs.[12] Contrast
"knowing where to look", that is, where one should look, with
"knowing where to find," that is, where one can find. It is quite
possible to do something otherwise than one should do it, so that
ignorance of how, or where, one should do it is no bar to doing it,

but at most only a bar to doing it as, or where, one should do it. This becomes clearer when one distinguishes between "being able to do something in some way or other" and "being able to do it correctly." Thus, the toastmaster who does not know how to address an Archbishop is able to address him, but not necessarily in the correct way, just as the visitor who does not know when to arrive is able to arrive, but not necessarily at the right time, or the plumber who does not know where to put in copper pipe is able to put it in, but not necessarily in the right place. On the other hand, it is not possible to do something other than one can do it, so that in so far as ignorance of how, or where, one can do it is a bar, it would be a bar both to doing it as, or where, one can do it and to doing it at all. But the question still remains whether knowing how, or where, one can V—and, *a fortiori*, knowing how or where, one should V—either implies or is implied by being able to V. And to this question I have already argued "No." Your ability to see things at a greater distance than I does not necessarily depend on your knowing how to do (or how one can do) this; nor does your knowing how to (or how one should) crochet necessarily enable you still to do it.

Again, though Brown suggests that not to know *where* to V implies not being able to V and, therefore, by contraposition, that being able to V implies knowing where to V, when the example of V is "find," the connection depends partly on what one finds. Perhaps Bo-peep couldn't find her sheep because she didn't know where to find them, but luckily not knowing where to find happiness does not necessarily make one unable to find it. Conversely, it makes no sense to say that water which is able to find its own level knows where or how to find it.

It is simply a mistake to suppose that the connection or lack of connection between "knowing how (or where) to" and "being able to" is due to different uses of the phrase "know how to." It is partly due to the type of thing one is able to do and to the type of agent. It is these features of Ryle's examples, not, as Brown supposes, any employment of an "English use," which account for the fact that they almost invariably show a connection between knowing how to V and being able to V.

Secondly, and more importantly, the connection between knowing how to run a projector, build a frame house—or to move about in a boat without upsetting it or to address a magistrate by his proper title—and being able to do these things is not a logical implication which would, therefore, depend either on the sense of "know how to" or on the sense of the words used to indicate what one knows how to do, but, as Brown half admits,[13] a causal relation which we saw also holds between being able to do such things as drive, swim, play chess or a cello and knowing how to do these. This is clear also from the fact that there is nothing logically absurd in the idea that machines—to which the idea of knowledge is inapplicable—might be constructed with the ability to run projectors and build houses as they already can be constructed with the ability to drive an engine, play chess or detect misprints. Many human successes, indeed, e.g., in detecting smells or distinguishing light from dark and loud from soft, result from instinct, not knowledge. Hence one cannot, as N. Brett[14] suggests, make the notion of success a *conceptual* explanation of why some abilities are related to know how and some are not.

Thirdly, Brown's suggested hypotheses about the deep grammar of the alleged two senses of "know how" are not supported by common examples. His first hypothesis is that "how to V" in the standard use indicates a or the *manner* in which to V and that in the alleged English use it indicates the *means*, method or procedure, of Ving. But there are many exceptions to this. For example, on this analysis, not knowing how to breathe, to hold six pints of beer or to blink would at one and the same time both be examples of the English use, since they are equivalent to not knowing the means or methods, rather than not knowing the manner, of doing these, and yet inconsistently also be examples of the standard use since they do not, as we saw, imply or even cause being unable to do these. Conversely, e.g., a child's not knowing how to behave properly at a funeral or a toastmaster's not knowing how to address an Archbishop would at one and the same time both be examples of the standard use, since they are equivalent to not knowing the manner in which to behave at a funeral or to address an Archbishop, and yet inconsistently also be examples of the English use, since such lack of knowledge would normally result in, even though it would not imply, the child's or the toastmaster's being unable to behave appropriate to the occasion.

Brown's second hypothesis, repeated in a later article,[15] is that to know how to V in the English use is to know *a* way to V, whereas to know how to V in the standard use is to know *the* way to V. But there are obvious exceptions to this hypothesis too. For example, not knowing how to spell a word, to extract square roots or to address an Archbishop makes one as little or as much unable to spell the word, extract square roots or address an Archbishop whether there is only one or several ways of doing these. Contrapositively, being able to breathe or to blink does not necessarily involve knowing how to breathe or to blink no manner how many ways there are of breathing or blinking.

Though "knowing how to" is the same wherever it occurs, there is, I agree with Brown, a difference between "knowing how to V" and "knowing how to F" which can be characterised as the difference between "knowing how one should V" and "knowing how one can F." Equally, though "knowing the way to"—which is a paraphrase of "knowing how to"—is the same wherever it occurs, there is, as Brown points out, a difference between "knowing the manner in which to V" and "knowing the means by which to F." This is, as I have suggested, indicated by the fact that "V" is usually replaceable by a "task" verb and "F" by an "achievement" verb. What one knows is the manner in which to carry out a task and the means by which to bring off an achievement. But neither of these differences shows, as Brown thinks, either a difference in two senses of "knowing how to" or that one of these uses, namely "knowing how to F," is implied, while the other, namely "knowing how to V," is not implied, by "being able to."

In order to evaluate Ryle's first thesis, namely that knowing how to do something is essentially different from—or is, as others[16] allege, a different kind of knowledge from—knowing that something is so, I shall now suggest a positive account of knowing how to V and attempt to counter his reasons for separating it from knowing that.

To know how to do something, whether this is something of a certain sort, such as how to play chess or the cello, to swim or to drive, to wink or breathe under water, or to extract gas from coal, or something particular, such as how to spell the word "silhouette," to open this tin or to get from Hull to Oxford by train, is to know the way to do it, just as to know when or where to do something is to know the time or place to do it, to know whom to do something to is to know the person to whom to do it, and to know what to do is to know the thing to do. And if such and such is the way, the time or the place to do it, the person to whom to do it or the thing to do, then to know how, when or where to do so and so, to know whom to do it to or to know what to do is to know that such and such is the way, time or place to do so and so, the person to whom to do it or is the thing to do. Furthermore, the "way" to do something covers the manner, means, method, etc., of doing it, and, therefore, covers both knowing how to perform a task and how to bring off an achievement.

Now Ryle need not and should not deny much or any of this. Certainly, in introducing the notion of knowing how to do something he explicitly equates it with "the discovery of the ways and methods of doing things"[17] and he frequently stresses that these ways and methods, e.g., of speaking French, arguing logically, playing chess or playing the cello, include "principles, rules, reasons, criteria." Whether or not he would allow the comparison of "knowing how to V" with "knowing when, where, what or whom to V" is more debatable, but there is not, I believe, any good reason for not doing so even on his own analysis of knowing how to. What Ryle does deny is that knowing how *to do* something— and possibly knowing when or where to do something, knowing what or whom to do—is the same kind of knowledge as knowing how—or when, where, what, who or that—something *is*.

The main reason for the denial is the false assimilation of the distinction between knowing how to and knowing that to two other distinctions which primarily interested him.

Ryle's main objective in his discussion of knowing how and knowing that was to draw attention to at least two important distinctions which in practice we ordinarily make, namely, first, the distinction between being stupid or clever and being ignorant or knowledgeable and, secondly, the distinction between being able to apply certain ways and methods of doing things or to act in accordance with certain principles, maxims and rules and being able to state what are these ways and methods or these principles, maxims and rules. He particularly wished to show that the first

alternative of each pair was not something "introduced and somehow steered by" the second element of its pair. Indeed, both his
main discussions, to the Aristotelian Society and in the *Concept of
Mind,* of the differences between knowing how to and knowing
that open with the announced intention of examining a set of
concepts—such as "clever," "logical," "wise," "prudent"—
which he calls "intelligence-concepts." Chastising his opponents
for allegedly taking knowing that as "the ideal model of all opera-
tions of intelligence" he claimed to have proved that "our intelli-
gence-predicates are definable in terms of knowing-how." But
even if this claim was correct, it would not show that knowing how
is explicable by intelligence concepts. So he frequently assumes
that his conclusions about intelligence are conclusions about
knowing how to, e.g., that to manifest one's knowledge how is to
exercise one's skill, that because one's skill in a certain art is
exhibited in what one does in it, not in what one says about it,
therefore so is one's knowledge of it, or that to know how to do
something is to be good at it.

But, first, the distinction between knowing or not knowing how
to do something and knowing or not knowing that something is so
is not the distinction between being clever or stupid and being
knowledgeable or ignorant. I am not necessarily stupid because I
don't know how to play chess or the cello, because I don't know
how to extract square roots or to pilot an aeroplane or because I
don't know how to open this tin lid or how to get from Aberystwyth
to Scarborough by train. Nor am I necessarily clever, logical,
intelligent or methodical because I know how to spell "cat," to
open a tin of beans or to play Ludo. Conversely, to confess my
complete ignorance of Serbo-Croat or the differential calculus, of
canasta or lacrosse is to admit that I do not know how to do certain
sorts of things. And many men are considered clever because they
have a lot of erudite information. Further, though intelligence, wit,
prudence, shrewdness, etc., may be characteristics of the way we
act, knowing how to act is not.

This assimilation of knowing how and intelligence gains some of
its plausibility from concentrating on examples of knowing how to
do things of a certain sort, e.g., play chess, argue logically, ride a
bicycle or speak grammatically, since it requires intelligence to fit

one's knowledge of a method or way to varying individual cases. Such an assimilation is much less plausible when the knowledge is how to do something unique, e.g., spell "silhouette," get from Hull to Whitby or light the grill on this cooker. Yet it would be unconvincing to argue that "know how to" changes its sense as the scope of the verb in the infinitive changes.

As regards the second distinction, there is an undoubted and important difference between being able to use certain ways and methods or apply certain rules or principles and being able to say what these ways and methods, rules and principles are, so that a man could, and often does, possess either one of these abilities without the other. But both abilities are forms which can in suitable circumstances be taken by knowing the ways and methods, the principles or rules, of doing things, that is, knowing *how* to do the things of which these are the ways and methods, the principles and rules, and neither ability is the same as the ability to do the things themselves.

It is because both being able to use a way or method of doing something and being able to state it are forms which knowing the way or method takes that someone who wishes to know how to do something can sometimes be shown how, sometimes be told how, and sometimes be both shown and told. I usually either show or tell someone how to open a tin, cook fish or get from the university to the motorway; I show him how to play the cello, shoot straight, ride a horse or pronounce the French word "feuille", and I tell him how to address an Archbishop, tell the age of articles of silver from their hallmarks or avoid paying tax on his earnings as a visiting professor to the United States. Now, I cannot normally show you how to pronounce a word without pronouncing it, demonstrate the way to address an Archbishop without uttering the address or exemplify how to play chess without playing. It is because showing someone how to do something normally involves doing it that being unable to do it implies being unable to show someone how to do it and, therefore, if showing how to do it were the only way in which knowing how to do it were manifested, it would also imply not knowing how to do it. Ryle, indeed, frequently suggests that the primary, maybe the exclusive, proof that, e.g., a school boy knows how to play chess is his being able to do it and that his merely being able to say how to do it is insufficient.[18] But not only is being able to tell us how to do something often not merely a sufficient, but also the usual, criterion of knowing how to do it, e.g., open a tin, find a chemist open in the middle of the night, or get to the motorway, it is, as we saw earlier, the only resource left to the crippled driving instructor, the paralysed swimming coach and the arthritic seamstress who wish to pass on their knowledge. The professor who confesses, perhaps to himself, that he has for the moment forgotten how to get into the Arts Building at the weekend or to castle in chess is not so much confessing that he is unable to do these as that he is unable to think how to do them. Equally, when he suddenly remembers how to do them or realises how to achieve his end by some other means, what he primarily does is to think of a or the way of doing them and only secondarily become equipped with the ability to do them. Contrariwise, merely being able to do something does not, as we saw, imply knowing how to do it, nor, indeed, does it imply being able to show someone how to do it. I don't by breathing, blinking or holding six pints of liquid, show anyone *how* to do these things, which I am able to do without knowing how.

Certainly, if what I claim to know how to do is something which someone can normally be both shown and told how to do, then my inability to show him how to do it by doing it will throw grave doubt on my claim unless I can produce some other extenuating disability. And, further, as Ryle emphasises, being able to show how to do something, e.g., to use the subjunctive mood, play chess or crack jokes, does not presuppose being able to tell anyone, even oneself, how to do it. Nor, of course, *vice versa*. But it is just as implausibly extreme to suggest that the scholar who is able to tell us exactly how to use the optative mood in Greek does not know how to use it just because he is not able to use it as well as a Greek child as it would be to suggest that the child who is able to use it but not to tell us how to use it does not know its use. There are many reasons why one of these abilities is not necessarily accompanied by the other, but none of these reasons, including stupidity, illogicality, foolishness or lack of intelligence is, as Ryle supposes, the same as lack of knowledge how. Further, as Ryle himself emphasises, knowing how (or where or when or who or what or that) something *is* can also involve showing and doing as well as telling. So that we are reluctant[19] to attribute knowledge, e.g., of time, place, date, person way or properties to the man who tells us the right answer but does not or cannot act appropriately. We normally take success in action as proof of knowledge that as well as of knowledge how. Knowing what colour something is can be as well exemplified by distinguishing it from others as by saying what colour it is and, as Ryle himself notes elsewhere, knowing how a tune goes is being able to recognise it, reproduce it, etc.

There is, moreover, an important reason why the ability to show someone how to do something—and, therefore, the ability to do it—is logically prior to the ability to tell him how to do it in an analysis of knowing how to do it. The reason is that what is known here is how *to do* something, the way or method of *doing* it, as contrasted with knowing how it *is*. But just as doing something is not itself showing how to do it, the ability to do it is not itself an ability to show how to do it, even though the former may be presupposed by the latter. And it is the ability to show how to do something, not the ability to do it, which is a, perhaps the primary, criterion of knowing how to do it.

A minor reason[20] for Ryle's contrast of knowing how and knowing that is his concentration on knowing how to do things of a certain sort as contrasted with specific things; a concentration perhaps understandable in one whose main interest was in human skills, accomplishments, proficiencies, expertise, etc. We saw earlier that this probably underlies his assimilation of knowing how with intelligence. It re-appears in his contention[21] that knowing how, but not knowing that, admits of degrees. For here he uses a general example for the former, but a specific example for the latter. But, though, admittedly, one cannot partly know that Napoleon lost the Battle of Waterloo as one can partly know French, one equally cannot partly know how to spell "deceive," whereas one can partly know the history of the Napoleonic Wars. And one can know very or perfectly well either how to play a cello or to pronounce "chaos" or that "illiterate" has two ll's. This one-sided diet of examples of knowing how to do things of a certain sort, rather than specific things, also accounts for his mistaken view that learning how to do something is different from learning that something is so. Though what we learn when we learn how to do something is not what we learn when we learn how or that something is so, learning how to do something is not necessarily, as Ryle suggests, improving an ability nor necessarily different from acquiring information. Though this may be true of learning how to play chess, to speak French, to extract square roots or to ride a bicycle, when I learn how to decrease the petrol consumption of my car, e.g., by fitting a new gadget, or how to get into a concert without paying, I have acquired fresh information, not improved my ability. And, further, the knowledge gained in these cases can be, and usually is, *contra* Ryle, imparted not inculcated, learned by being told, not by practice.

Having tried to refute Ryle's main arguments for denying that knowing how to do something and knowing that something is so are essentially the same kind of knowledge, I want to conclude with some of the basic similarities between the two.

Knowing how *to do* something—or when or where to do it, whom to do it to or even what to do—differs, I suggest, from knowing how something *is*—or when, where, who, what or that it is—not as a different kind of knowledge, but merely as knowledge of a different kind of thing, just as knowing the way *to do* something—or the time or place to do it, the person to do it to or even the thing to do—differs from knowing the way something *is*—or the place, time, person or character it is, or merely that it is—as knowledge of different kinds of things, not as different kinds of knowledge.

We can learn, find out, remember or forget, tell or be told, show or be shown, how to tie a reef knot, when to press a switch or where to make an incision, just as we can learn, find out, remember or forget, tell or be told, show or be shown, how our muscles work, when wood worm breed or where ground nuts are grown. Furthermore, belief operates similarly with knowing how to do something and with knowing how something is. Though we can believe that something is so, we can no more believe how, where, when, what or who something is, than we can believe how, when or where to do something, whom to do something to or what to do. And we can as equally believe that this is how, (where, when, etc.) to do something as that this is how (where, when, etc.) it is. Admittedly, we cannot ask someone for the grounds or reasons for his knowledge how, but neither can we ask this of his knowledge that. But we can be as uncertain or unsure how, when, where or what to do as we can how, when, where or what it is.

To know something is, I shall later suggest, to have the answer to a possible question, whether it is the question what to do, how, when or where to do it or whom to do it to or whether it is what, how, when, where or who so and so is. To have this answer is to be able to produce it, just as to have patience, wisdom, insight, tact, flexibility or magnetism is to be able to display these. And the two forms which the ability to produce the answer to a question take are, as I have mentioned, the ability to *say* what the answer is and the ability to *show* what it is. These two forms are logically and practically independent, so that we can say what the answer is without, for various reasons, being able to show what it is and can show what it is without, for different reasons, being able to say what it is. In general, though by no means invariably or necessarily, the ability to show what the answer is goes with knowledge of how (or where, when, what, who) *to do* and the ability to say what it is with knowledge of how (or when, where, who, what or that) it *is*.

Knowing how to do something and knowing how or that something is are not, therefore, two kinds of knowledge, but knowledge of two kinds of things. It is simply a mistake to assert that knowledge how to do something is not to possess knowledge at all, but to be intelligent. Knowledge of both kinds of things is an ability, but knowledge of how to do something is not the ability to do the thing itself, but the ability either to show or to tell how to do it. The ability to do the thing itself is simply a consequence and, therefore, a proof of the ability to show how to do it. That a person tends or is able to do certain things well, correctly or efficiently, is not, as Ryle asserts, what we mean by describing him as knowing *how* to talk grammatically, to play chess or to fish. The former arises because of the latter.

C. AN INTERROGATIVE WITH "KNOW"

Quite different from "know" followed by an interrogative is "know" preceded by an interrogative. An interrogative which precedes "know" does not indicate the object of knowledge, the thing known, but something about the circumstances in which it is known. Thus, we can distinguish between the preceding interrogative "When, where, why or how did you know?" and the following interrogative "Did you know when, where, why or how?" in that the former asks about a particular object of knowledge, e.g., the date of the Battle of the Boyne, that there is no life after death, the new Minister of Defence or how to tune a carburettor, what was the time, place, circumstances or cause of your knowledge of it, whereas the latter asks whether you had any knowledge about the time, place, circumstances or cause of something. Hence, one can use both interrogatives together, as in "How did you know how to do it?" or "When did you know when it happened?."

D. "KNOW" WITH A QUASI-INTERROGATIVE

Of the various, importantly different, ways in which we state in English our knowledge of something by means of the verb "to know" followed by a noun, two are variations on "know" with an interrogative.

(I) "KNOW" THE COLOUR, WEIGHT . . . .

In the first the noun indicates the *identity* of what is known. Thus, to know the colour, shape, size, weight, date, cause, result, name, etc., of something is to know *what* is its colour, shape, size, etc., and hence, to know *that* it is such and such. In an analogous way, to suspect foul play, fear a hiding or advise a return to work is to suspect or fear that there is such or to advise that there be such. Hence, there is no suggestion in the ordinary use, as contrasted with Russell's[22] unidiomatic use, of, e.g., "knowing the colour of someone's curtains," that we have had any direct contact with what we know, that we have seen the colour of the curtains. Conversely, it does not follow that because we have, e.g., seen the colour of the curtains, we, therefore, know their colour. Knowing the colour of someone's curtains because one has seen them is acquiring one's knowledge of their colour by a different means from acquiring it by hearsay or by being told, but there is no reason to suppose that the knowledge one has acquired is any different or that what one has acquired it of is any different. Similarly, to know someone's feelings on a particular matter or to know the pain that something caused him is to know what are his feelings or what is the pain. It is not, *per impossibile,* to experience his feelings or his pain or even to experience similar sympathetic feelings or pains of one's own. Plato, like Russell, may have been misled by this use of a noun for an interrogative after "know" into thinking that knowledge is sometimes a direct acquaintance with objects. Thus, our knowledge of, e.g., (the Form of) Equality is expressed by Plato as our "knowing it, what it is."[23]

(II) "KNOW FRENCH, ...

The second case in which the use of "know" with a noun conceals an interrogative is that in which the noun indicates something we can learn or know *how* to speak, recite or calculate, e.g., French, the Rime of the Ancient Mariner or the twelve times table. We have already analysed the meaning of "know how to V."

E. "KNOW" WITH A RELATIVE

The pronouns "who" and "what," unlike "where," "when," "why" or "how," can be used both interrogatively and relatively to introduce an object of knowledge. "Whom or what did you know?" asks which persons or things were known to you, whereas "Did you know who or what . . . " asks whether you knew which persons or things are so and so. The grammatical difference between "who" and "whom," which is concealed in "what," clearly brings out that what is known in "Whom did you know?" is a person, whereas in "Did you know who . . . ?" it is the answer to the question "Who . . . ?." Though the "what" which follows "know" is usually interrogative, as in "He knows what was said last night in the House of Commons," it is sometimes relative, as in "He already knew what I began to tell him." "Know" followed by a relative pronoun always takes the indicative mood and is clearly only a variation either for knowing some fact, e.g., that p or what or where or when or how something is—as when I already knew what he was telling me—or for knowing some person—as when A is someone whom I know.

The grammatical difference between the interrogative "what" and the relative "what" is, we shall see, an important clue in the problem, first raised in Plato's *Republic,* whether what is believed and what is known can be the same. For, though one can both believe and know what is said in the Bible, it does not follow from this that what one believes and what one knows is the same, since the "what" in "believing what is said" is relative, whereas the "what" in "knowing what is said" is interrogative. This is why one can know, but not believe, what it is that was said, and why one can believe, but not know, whatever another says. More importantly, if it is said in the Bible that the world was created in six days, then someone who believes what is said in the Bible would believe that the world was created in six days; but someone who knew what was said in the Bible would not necessarily know that the world was created in six days, but only that the Bible says it was. Similarly, if one has been taught, incorrectly, that Columbus discovered America in 1592, one who believes what he was taught believes that Columbus discovered America in 1592, but one who remembers what he was taught does not—because he cannot—remember that Columbus discovered America in 1592. Furthermore,[24] one can be taught and, perhaps, learn that p without knowing that p because one can be taught and, perhaps, learn what is false or what is not so, though one cannot know what is false or what is not so. Plato[25] was mistaken in arguing that "a man is not taught anything but knowledge."

The difference between the relative and the interrogative "what" also throws light on a puzzle about our knowledge of other people.[26] It is often thought that because I can feel what I feel, e.g., tiredness or depression, but not feel what you feel, therefore, though I know what I feel, I cannot know what you feel. But when I feel what I feel and fail to feel what you feel, "what" is relative and refers to that which you feel and I either feel or fail to feel, whereas when I know what I feel or know what you feel, "what" is interrogative and refers to what it is that I know. Hence, there is not something which it is alleged I can both know and feel in myself, but not know, because I cannot feel, in you. I know what it is I feel because I feel it, whereas I know what it is you feel other than by feeling it.

F. "KNOW THAT"

"Know" is commonly followed by a that-nominalisation, as when one knows that it is raining, that water boils at 100° Centigrade or that the Battle of the Boyne was fought in 1690. The use of "know" with an infinitive, as in "knowing a student to be hard working, a payment to be overdue or a proposition to be true or false," is only a grammatical variation—common, for example, in Latin—on this. I have also argued that all the other constructions with "know" discussed above can be reduced to "knowing that." That, for instance, to know where to find the missing spanner is to know that so and so is the place to find it, that to know when A will arrive is to know that he will arrive at such and such a time, that to know the colour of the curtains is to know that so and so is their colour, that to know how to cook aubergines is to know that the way to cook them is such and such and that to know one's twelve times tables is to know for each number from one to twelve that so and so or such and such is the product of any two of these numbers. Furthermore, the knowledge expressed in English by "knowing that" has throughout the history of philosophy been so much regarded as the central case of knowledge that most analyses, tests, criteria and conditions of knowledge have been formulated with almost sole regard to it. Hence, any examination of the "objects of knowledge" must ask what is it that one knows when one knows that p.

Most analyses of knowledge that p have been based on the assumption that what is known here is the *proposition* that p.[27] Hence, this knowledge has frequently been called 'propositional knowledge' just as an analogous assumption that to believe, feel, hope, suspect or wish that p is to believe, feel, hope, suspect or wish the proposition that p has led philosophers to follow Russell in calling belief, fear, hope, suspicion, wishing, etc., "propositional attitudes."

Philosophers have rarely given any argument for their view that what is known when it is known that p is the proposition that p because this followed from the other thesis of theirs that what is believed when it is believed that p is the proposition that p—as what is hoped, feared, wished, etc., when it is hoped, feared, wished, etc., that p is the proposition that p—together with the assumption that what is known and what is believed when it is known and believed that p are the same. I shall discuss both this other thesis and this assumption later. Here it will be sufficient to argue briefly and independently that it is a mistake to suppose that what is known when it is known that p is the proposition that p.

First, to say that what is known when one knows that p is a proposition cannot mean what is ordinarily meant when it is said that one knows a proposition, e.g., the proposition about pleasure which Aristotle attributed to Plato, for to know the proposition that p in this, the ordinary, sense does not imply that one knows that p, since the proposition one knows could be a false proposition. A well known proposition can be mistaken; but if it is well known that p, it canot fail to be that p. To know a proposition, in the ordinary sense, is either to know what proposition it is or to be acquainted with it. Indeed, I shall argue shortly that underlying the view that what is known—like what is believed, suspected, feared, advised, etc.,—when it is known—or believed, etc.,—that p is the proposition that p is an assimilation of two kinds of accusatives of the verb "know"—"believe," etc.,—namely the kind that occurs when one knows or believes a person or a proposition and the kind that occurs when one knows or believes that p. Secondly, it is quite common for philosophers who suppose that "knowing that p" is knowing the proposition that p to confuse the latter with "knowing that the proposition that p is true." Frequently, indeed, they hop about between talk of knowing propositions and talk of knowing propositions to be true.[29] But to know that the proposition that p is true is no more the same as to know the proposition that p than to know that the proposition that p is false is to know the proposition that p or than to know that the gearbox is faulty is to know the gearbox. Similarly, to know the proposition to be true is no more to know the proposition than to know the gearbox to be faulty is to know the gearbox. Furthermore, what is known when one knows that the proposition that p is true is not that p. For, if the proposition that p were a proposition which one did not understand, one could know that the proposition that p is true—e.g., if one had been told on good authority that this strange proposition were true—without knowing that p and one could know that p—e.g., by discovering it for oneself—without knowing that this strange proposition, which is the proposition that p, is true.

Thirdly, the view that knowing that p is knowing the proposition that p is due to a misunderstanding about the place that truth occupies in knowledge and belief and to a confusion between what is true and what is so. Knowledge is often distinguished from belief on the ground that what is believed can be true or false, but what is known can only be true. Since it is propositions which can be either true or false and propositions which can be only true, it is concluded that what is known or believed must be a proposition. But there is a confusion here. The fact that the truth of the proposition "He believes that p" does not depend, while the truth of the proposition "He knows that p" does depend, on the truth of the proposition that p does not show that what he believes when he believes that p and what he knows when he knows that p is something which can be true, namely a proposition, anymore than the fact that the truth of the proposition "He fears that p" does not depend, while the truth of the proposition "He discovers that p" does depend, on the truth of the proposition that p shows that what he fears when he fears that p and what he discovers when he discovers that p is something that can be true, namely a proposition. Certainly, something can be believed to be true without being true, though not known to be true without being true. But this no more shows that what can be known must always be the sort of thing that can be true, that is a proposition, than the fact that something can be believed to be lost without being lost, though not known to be lost without being lost, shows that what can be known must always be the sort of thing that can be lost. The confusion between knowing or believing something to be so and knowing or believing something to be true is no doubt due to the fact that it is true that p if and only if p. But what is true, namely (the proposition) that p, is not what makes it true, namely (the fact) that p. The alleged platitude that if someone knows that p, then it is true that p is a platitude not because what is known is a true proposition, but because if someone knows that p, then it is a fact that p and if it is a fact that p, then it is true (to say) that p.

A fourth mistake of philosophers who suppose that to know—or to believe, suspect, etc.,—that p is to know—or believe, suspect, etc.,—the proposition that p is to conclude that because what is known—believed, suspected, etc.,—is *expressed by* a proposition, therefore what is known—believed, suspected, etc.,—*is* a proposition.[31] For somewhat similar and some additional reasons,[32] it is even less plausible to suppose that what is known—believed, suspected, etc.,— when one knows—believes, suspects, etc.,— that p are the words "that p" or the sentence "p."

We must, therefore, distinguish knowing that p from knowing the proposition that p (or the sentence "p") and, hence, what is known when one knows the former from what is known when one knows the latter. What, then, is it that is known when one knows that p?

To answer this we must distinguish between what I shall call the "object-accusative" and the "nominalisation-accusative" of a verb. Thus, to say that one suspects the butler, diagnoses a patient, doubts a man's word, fears a bully, advises a trade union, believes in one's party, asks the porter, teaches John, knows Simon, is aware of a mouse or displays a banner, is to indicate—as does "play the ball"—the object towards which one's attitude, ability, action, etc., is directed. By contrast, to say that one suspects foul play, diagnoses tuberculosis, doubts the wisdom of a plan, fears a hiding, advises a return to work, believes in fairies, asks the time, teaches a solution, knows the date, is aware of the difficulties or displays anger, is not to indicate any relation of the subject of the verb to some existent or, *per impossibile,* some non-existent object, whether foul play, fairies or a historical date, much less to a substitute object, such as a proposition or concept. It is to characterise—as does, e.g., "play ball (chess or cards)"—the nature of one's attitude, action, ability or whatever. It is to indicate what it amounts to. The latter form of words, unlike the former, is a variation on a "that-nominalisation." Hence, suspecting foul play, diagnosing tuberculosis, advising a return to work, believing in fairies, asking the time, knowing the date, being aware of the difficulties and displaying anger is suspecting that there has been foul play, diagnosing that there is tuberculosis, advising that there should be a return to work, believing that there are fairies, asking what is the time, knowing that the date is so and so, being aware that there are such and such difficulties and displaying that one is angry. By contrast, suspecting the butler, diagnosing a patient, advising a trade union, believing in one's party, asking the porter, knowing Simon, being aware of a mouse and displaying a banner is not suspecting that there is a butler, diagnosing that there is a patient, advising that there be a trade union, believing that there is one's party, asking what is the porter, knowing that there is Simon, being aware that there is a mouse or displaying that there is a banner. Implausible as it is to suppose that, e.g., foul play, a return to work or the date of a battle is something to which I may direct my suspicion, advice or knowledge, it is even more implausible to suppose that I might direct one of these to something bewilderingly called "that there has been foul play," "that there should be a return to work" or "that 1690 is the date of the battle." It is failure to see this implausibility which led philosophers to suppose that these phrases must be the names of propositions or facts and that these are what I suspect, advise or know. Knowing the time is related to knowing the porter as asking the time is to asking the porter. To know the time is to know what time it is as to ask the time is to ask what time it is; neither is a relation between someone and the time, much less between him and something called "what the time is."

One consequence of this difference is that the object-accusative must signify something which exists and towards which one can react in the named way, whereas the existence of what is signified by the nominalisation-accusative depends on the nature of the verb. The nominalisation-accusative of intentional verbs, like suspect, diagnose, doubt, fear, advise, believe in, ask, can signify what does not exist. One can suspect foul play when there is none or give advice which no one takes or ask the time of a meeting which has been cancelled. By contrast, the nominalisation-accusative of non-intentional verbs, like know, be aware or display, must signify what does exist. One cannot know the wrong date, be aware of non-existent dangers or display an anger which one has not got. But the nominalisation-accusative of even a non-intentional verb, such as "know," differs as regards existence from the object-accusative. What the object-accusative, e.g., the porter, signifies, is something which can cease to exist and which, therefore, we can be said to have known, but not still to know, even though we remember him well. The nominalisation-accusative, on the other hand, does not indicate a sort of object which exists for awhile and then ceases to exist. Hence, to say that we used to know, e.g., the time, but no longer know it, implies that we have forgotten it, not that it has ceased to exist. Similarly, to tell a policeman that the person who attacked you is someone you used to know is to treat the attacker as an object of your knowledge, whereas to tell the policeman that you would know your attacker again is to treat "attacker" as a nominalisation-accusative.

Another consequence of the difference between object-accusatives and nominalisation-accusatives is that we can say that, when I suspect foul play or that there is foul play, then foul play or that there is foul play is my suspicion, but we cannot say that, when I suspect the butler, then the butler is my suspicion; and we can say that when I know the date of the battle or that the date of the battle is 1690, then the date of the battle or that the date is 1690 is part of my knowledge, but we cannot say that, when I know Simon, then he is part of my knowledge. This is the same difference as that between saying rightly that tuberculosis is my diagnosis or that my advice is a return to work and saying wrongly that the patient is my diagnosis or that my advice is a trade union.

If you know the porter and the porter is the shop steward of the local trade union, then you know the shop steward of the local trade union, even if you do not know (or even think) that you know him; whereas you can know the time of the bus without knowing the time of the train, even though the time of the bus is the same as the time of the train. For, if you know X and X is also Y, then you know Y; but if you know what X is, e.g., Z, and X is also Y, it does not follow that you know what Y is.

Other modern languages distinguish between our knowing the porter and our knowing the time by using different verbs for "know." Thus, French uses "connaître" and German "kennen" when the "object of knowledge" is expressed by an object-accusative, but "savoir" and "wissen" when it is expressed by a nominalisation-accusative. So, to know the porter is "connaître le concierge" or "kennen den Hausmeister" while to know the time is "savoir le temps" or "wissen die Uhr."

Again, a list of what one knows, like a list of what one suspects, advises or asks, would contain things referred to by nominalisation—accusatives, but not by object-accusatives. A list of what one knows includes dates, results, causes, properties, etc., but not places, buildings, experiences or people, just as a list of what one suspects includes crimes and moves, but not motives or people, a list of what one advises includes actions, withdrawals and settlements, but not corporations, governments or people, and a list of what one asks is comprised of questions, but not of people or committees.

The moral to be drawn from all this is that the philosophical title "Objects of knowledge" refers to two disparate lists, a list of what one knows—e.g., that p, what, where, when, how or who V's, or what, where, when, whom or how to V, and all those things to know which is to know what they are (e.g., dates, causes, colours, etc.)—and a list of people and things, whether places or conditions, with which one is acquainted. Similarly, the "object" of belief can be divided into those things which go to characterise one's belief, e.g., that p, in fairies, and those in which one puts one's trust, e.g., stories, people. In the former we do not have—as we do in the latter—a relation between a believer and an object, but a belief of a certain kind.[33] It is a philosophical mistake to suppose that the items on the former list are "objects" in the same sense as those on the latter and, *a fortiori*, to suppose that they are peculiar objects called "propositions." Propositions, whether known or believed, are on the latter list. Well known propositions are in this respect like well known people and places. It would, however, be a mistake of the opposite kind to suppose that because, e.g., "suspect," "believe," "fear" or "know" or, far less plausibly, "diagnose," "advise," "display" can take different kinds of objects and, hence, occur in statements with different implications, therefore they are themselves used in different senses and, hence, that the knowledge we have in knowing, e.g., a person is different from that in knowing, e.g., a date or, far less plausibly, the advice we give in advising a trade union is different from that in advising a return to work. It is not the knowledge, any more than the belief, suspicion, fear, diagnosis or advice, which is different, but its "object."

G. KNOWLEDGE BY ACQUAINTANCE

We saw earlier that "know" can be followed by a noun to express an implicit interrogative, as in "knowing the colour of the curtains," that is, knowing what the colour is, or in "knowing French," that is, knowing how to speak French. It also frequently takes a noun to indicate somebody or something with which one is directly acquainted. This, as we saw, is a use for which some languages have special verbs, e.g. "connaître" in French, "kennen" in German and "conoscere" in Italian. It is in this way that we know places, persons or their productions, and various characteristics, conditions or states. We may know or not know our next door neighbour, the present Lord Mayor of our city, Orson Welles' production of *Macbeth* or Boswell's *Life of Johnson*. It is in this way that we speak of knowing or never having known such rudeness, stupidity, hatred, excitement or joy, such discomfort or hunger, such a case of diphtheria, inflation like the present, great pain or poverty. To assert how well we know a particular taste, smell or look is to express our familiarity with it. It is also in this way that someone's voice or face becomes well known, e.g., by being heard on the radio or on a record or being seen on the television or in the newspaper.

We date the beginning of our knowledge of these to the time and place where we "met," "came across," "encountered" or "experienced" them. We get to know people at school, in the navy or in middle age. When these things cease to exist, we cease to know them. So that we speak of "having known," but not "knowing," rudeness, pain or poverty. We cannot know people after they are dead, cities after they have been destroyed or poverty after we have become rich. Hence, knowing all about, or being able to recognise, something or somebody, much less knowing what or who he is, is not sufficient for knowing it or him, for we can know all about, but not in this way know, a historical, fictional or no longer existing person or place. Equally, knowing of a person or place, whether by repute, hearsay, etc., is not enough for knowing him or it. Since some of these things, such as people, places or productions, are very complex, we assess our knowledge of them as passing or superficial, intimate or familiar. We can know them inside out or like the back of our hand.

But, though making their direct acquaintance is necessary for knowing these things or persons, it is not sufficient. One does not know everyone one has met, every place one has been or everything one has experienced. One has to know something about them. And this knowledge can increase from a mere passing acquaintance to a deep and intimate familiarity. Wives usually know their husbands, natives their towns and critics their authors' works better than strangers do. and what they know is that and what, when, whom, why and how. Hence, the necessary means of acquiring this knowledge of something is not itself part of this knowledge, nor does its necessity give any reason for supposing that this is a different kind of knowledge or that it is knowledge in a different sense of that word. Knowledge by acquaintance is knowledge gained in a certain way, not knowledge of a certain kind. It is in fact the same kind of knowledge which might in theory, if not in practice, have been acquired differently.

Furthermore, what we know by acquaintance is, as we have seen, an "object of knowledge" in a different way from that in which what we know about it is an object. The former is not a bit of knowledge, but that about which we have some bit of knowledge.

What we know when we know something or somebody by acquaintance is not what we know when we know what that thing or person is, despite the fact that we can often express both of these in the same way in English, as when we talk, e.g., of knowing the heavyweight boxing champion of the world. For, if we know, by acquaintance, the heavyweight champion, then he is someone whom we know, whether or not we know that he is the heavyweight champion; but if we simply know the heavyweight champion in the sense that we know who is the champion, then he is not necessarily someone whom we know. Furthermore, the man *whom* we know is not *what* we know. What we know is the answer to the question "Who is the heavyweight champion?." If, on being attacked, I told the police that I used to know my attacker, this would be a claim to knowledge by acquaintance, but if I told them that I would know him again if I saw him, this would be a claim to be able to recognise him.

Knowing the heavyweight champion in the sense of knowing who is the heavyweight champion is no different from knowing, e.g., the answer, result, date, cause, weight, etc., of something, where clearly there is no implication that we know these things by acquaintance. Knowing the champion by acquaintance, on the other hand, carries no implication of what or how much we know of him, not even that we know that he is the champion. The difference between knowing, by acquaintance, the heavyweight champion and knowing (who is) the heavyweight champion is, as we saw, parallel to that between, e.g., suspecting the butler and suspecting foul play, fearing the teacher and fearing a hiding, advising a trade union and advising a return to work.

This everyday distinction between what we know by acquaintance and what we know other than by acquaintance is not the same as Russell's technical distinction between "knowledge by acquaintance" and "knowledge by description". For Russell thought of "knowledge by acquaintance" and "knowledge by description" as two ways of knowing things or two kinds of knowledge. First, he considered both as giving a relation between the knower and the known, which differed in that the former relation was immediate and direct, while the latter was inferential and indirect. Secondly, he thought that in theory the same thing could, at least in some cases, be known in both ways. Thirdly, he thought that to know something by acquaintance was simply to be aware of it and that A's awareness of X was simply X's being present to A. Hence, we are strictly "acquainted" with something only while it is "before us" in perception, memory or thought. Russell's use of "acquaintance", however, is equivalent neither to the ordinary use of "acquaintance" nor to the ordinary uses of any of the expressions, such as "awareness," "consciousness," "notice" or "experience" with which he at various times identified it.[34] He considered knowing the colour, shape, size or smell of something to be examples of knowledge by acquaintance; whereas they usually are really examples of what is in the ordinary sense knowledge other than by acquaintance, though in, e.g., "How well I know that colour, smell, sound"—as in "that scent, name, time"—they could also be objects of acquaintance. Conversely, he considered knowing the object (or person) which had this colour, shape, size or smell to be knowledge other than by acquaintance, whereas it is often what is in the ordinary sense knowledge by acquaintance.

A danger of Russell's view of knowledge by acquaintance, as of Plato's view of the knowledge of Forms, is that it misleads us into thinking that *what* is known is an object with which we have a peculiar direct relation called "knowledge"—and that *what* is believed is an object with which we have a relation called "belief"—whereas, I have argued, what is known—like what is believed—is the content of our knowledge or belief. The people, places, conditions we are acquainted with, like the people whose word we accept, are, perhaps, something we could be said to have a relation to; but they are not the "objects" of our knowledge or belief.

What we know when we know the porter, like what we suspect, advise or diagnose, when we suspect, advise or diagnose the porter, is what our knowledge, like our suspicion, advice or diagnosis, is *directed* to; whereas what we know when we know the time, like what we suspect when we suspect foul play, what we advise when we advise a return to work or what we diagnose when we diagnose tuberculosis, is what our knowledge, like our suspicion, advice or diagnosis, *amounts* to. These are two different questions about the same thing, whether knowledge, suspicion, advice or diagnosis, not the same question about two different things.

CHAPTER THREE

Extent of Knowledge

A. INTRODUCTION

Philosophers of all ages have taken as one purpose of their examination of the nature of knowledge that which Locke characterised in the opening pages of his *Essay* as "to enquire into the original, certainty and extent of human knowledge." By the "extent of knowledge" they meant, not how much we actually do know—the answers to which it is the business of an encyclopaedia to collect— but how much we can know. And this is a question whose answer depends on what kind of a thing knowledge is.

Common to most philosophers bent on determining the extent of knowledge is an assumption, at least as old as Plato, which Locke expressed in his immediately subsequent paragraph as "It is, therefore, worth while to search out the bounds between opinion and knowledge." Most philosophers have held that the area of what can be known is a segment of the area of what can be believed, being distinguished from the whole either as what must be true or as what must be necessary or as what must be certain. A few, however, have held that knowledge and belief cover mutually exclusive areas. According to the former view, anything that can be known can be believed, but not everything that can be believed can be known; while according to the latter, neither can what can be believed be known nor can what can be known be believed.

Since there are, as far as I am aware, only two sustained arguments in the history of philosophy for the latter view, let us consider it first.

B. CAN WHAT IS KNOWN AND WHAT IS BELIEVED BE THE SAME?

(I) PLATO'S ANSWER

At the end of the fifth book of the *Republic*,[1] Plato poses and gives a negative answer to the question "Can what is known and what is

45

believed be the same?." In this he is partly followed by Aristotle.[2] Plato's two main sets of reasons for this answer are (1) that knowledge and belief are different powers (δύναμις) and that powers differ only in what they do and in what they are powers over ('επι); (2) that what is known is what is, what is real and what is unchanging, whereas what is believed is between what is and what is not, is only appearance and is liable to change. Now, although the second set of reasons could be used and, we shall see, has been used by Hume and the Logical Positivists, to deny knowledge of much of what is believed, since they all suggest that what is believed could be deficient or wrong, it is difficult to see why the reasons should deny belief of what is known unless they are linked with the assumption in the first set of reasons that what is the object of one thing, e.g., of one power, cannot be the object of another. This assumption also underlies Plato's analogy of the Line in Book VI of the *Republic,* where a different mental capacity corresponds to each different type of object. Plato's adherence to this assumption may have been due to the influence of the two examples he gave of powers, namely that of sight and hearing, since it could be argued that what we see cannot be the same as what we hear, for what we see are colours and what we hear are sounds and we cannot see sounds or hear colours. We can, however, both see and hear bells and trains. Therefore, it would be necessary for proponents of this view to show that believing something and knowing something are analogous to seeing colours and hearing sounds and not to seeing and hearing bells and trains. And this, indeed, must be what is in the minds of those who argue, as we shall see, that what we believe are propositions and what we know are facts. Since, however, we can, as we shall mention, also believe and know the same thing, e.g., people and their stories, it would have to be shown that any other examples of believing and knowing share in one analogy rather than in the other. Furthermore, there are many abilities other than the ability to see and to hear which do not differ in their objects, e.g., the ability to push and to pull, to add and to subtract, to distinguish and to assimilate.

A quasi-psychological variant on Plato's, and Aristotle's, thesis is H. H. Price's argument[3] that we cannot know and believe the same thing, at least at the same time, for to know that A is B is to be in direct cognitive contact with it and to have it present to one's consciousness, whereas to believe it is at best to be only in indirect contact with it through the medium of the proposition that A is B and to have only the proposition present in consciousness. Because one cannot, it is said, have both these objects present to one's consciousness at once, one cannot know and believe something at the same time. This argument, however, stands or falls with the assumption, to be considered in the next section, that what one believes when one believes that A is B is the proposition that A is B.

(II) VENDLER'S ANSWER

A recent attempt to support Plato's conclusion has been made by Zeno Vendler in Chapter 5 of his book *Res Cogitans*.[4] As Plato thought of belief as pertaining only to the appearances or likenesses of things, but knowledge to the things themselves,[5] so Vendler concludes (p. 118) that "the immediate object of believing is . . . a picture of reality," while "the immediate object of knowing is . . . reality itself." While "knowledge is access to what is given; belief is the holding of an image." While what is believed is something that can be true or false—compare Plato's being and not-being—what is known is not (p. 113). While what is believed is a proposition, what is known is a fact. While what is believed is subjective, what is known is objective. Vendler's methods of supporting these conclusions are, however, quite different from Plato's.

Vendler's argument for his thesis is that "believe" is what he called a *subjective* verb and "know" what he called an *objective* verb. For this he gave two main criteria (1) that *subjective* verbs can take only "subjective that-clauses," by which he means *propositions*, whereas *objective* verbs can take only "objective that-clauses," by which he means *facts:* (2) that *subjective* verbs cannot take, whereas *objective* verbs can take, wh-nominalisations—in practice these are the interrogatives what, who, where, when, how—which Vendler also considers a mark of the objective.

Various writers, e.g., White,[6] Jones,[7] Dunn and Suter,[8] have shown that neither of these criteria is sufficient to distinguish the group of verbs which Vendler says are *subjective,* e.g., believe, say, anticipate, imagine, decide, suggest, confess, predict, suspect, assume, promise, testify, from the group of verbs which he says are *objective,* e.g., know, state, tell, find out, realise, learn, notice.

The first criterion is not valid because, despite some ungrounded protests from Vendler, it is perfectly good English to say, e.g., "A knows what B only suspects," "A (dis)proved what B assumed (predicted)" and "A believed what B told him," "A suspected what in fact happened," "I asserted all I knew," "Very few bishops believed what Darwin had discovered." I can believe what I see as easily as I can believe what you say. Furthermore, I can anticipate, assume, imagine, predict or suspect the result or outcome of something.

The second criterion is not valid because, though "say," "anticipate," "suspect," "suggest," "confess," "predict," are all what Vendler calls *subjective* verbs, we can say, anticipate, suspect, suggest, confess, predict where and when the treasure was hidden, who hid it and how he did so. Vendler may have been misled here by the fact that both "I say (anticipate, suggest, suggest, confess, predict)" and "A's statement (anticipation, suspicion, suggestion, confession, prediction) is" take only "that p" and not "wh . . .". But the reason for this is that these forms are used expressly to enunciate the statement (anticipation, etc.,), not merely to indicate indirectly its subject matter.

Though Vendler does not explicitly say so, his catalogue (pp. 117–18) of differences between knowing and believing themselves—e.g., "*How* do you know?" as contrasted with "*Why* do you believe?"—is relevant only on the assumption that it constitutes an additional subsidiary criterion for a difference between what is known and what is believed. But the assumption, made also by Plato,[9] that a difference between Ving and Fing implies a difference between what is Ved and what is Fed is, as we have just seen, mistaken.

In his book Vendler attempts to account for some exceptions to his thesis by distinguishing between the wh-nominalisation following "know," etc.,—which is said to be objective and non-interrogative—and that following, e.g., "wonder"—which is allowed to be

interrogative and subjective. Since, moreover, many alleged subjective verbs, e.g., "say," "suspect," etc., can take wh-nominalisation in negative sentences (e.g., "He did not say where he
went)," wh-nominalisation in negative sentences cannot, according to him, be allowed to be a sign of the objective. But it is most
implausible that what is not known should be subjective while
what is known should be objective. The same thing, e.g., why the
crime was committed, can at one time be not known and later
become known. Vendler tries to ease his conscience by suggesting
that, e.g., "I do not know that Joe stole the watch" is odd. But this
is no more odd than "We don't know that he did it." Nor is there
anything the least odd about, e.g., "I did not know until yesterday
that Joe had stolen the watch." Further, it is not only negatives,
but interrogatives (e.g., "Did you know . . . ?)," modals "(Can
one know . . . ?)," etc., which would have to be analysed in terms
of this second wh-nominalisation.

A second subsidiary criterion which Vendler uses in support of
his alleged difference between what is known and what is believed
is this. If someone believes a prediction and the prediction is that p,
then someone believes that p, whereas if someone knows a prediction and the prediction is that p, it does not follow that he knows
that p. But this difference in implication can be equally well explained without assuming that the *that p* which is known is different from the *that p* which is believed. The difference could equally
well be due to the fact that to believe a prediction implies, or
possibly even means, to believe that the prediction is correct,
whereas to know a prediction does not imply, nor mean, to know
that the prediction is correct. Since it follows that if a prediction
that p is correct, then what it predicts, namely that p, is the case,
then either to believe or to know that a prediction that p is correct
implies to believe or to know that it is the case that p. The reason
why we cannot argue from knowing the prediction that p to knowing that p, while we can argue from believing the prediction that p
to believing that p could be that knowing the prediction does not
imply knowing it to be correct as believing it does imply believing it
to be correct. This would explain why, e.g., "suspect"—though a
subjective verb according to Vendler—behaves here like "know."
One cannot argue that because I suspect his story and his story is

that p, therefore I suspect that p. It also explains why, on the other hand, e.g., "admit" ("prove")—though an objective verb according to Vendler—behaves like "believe." To admit (prove) his story that p is to admit (prove) that p because to admit (prove) his story is to admit (prove) it to be true. Contrariwise, if the fact, cause, result, etc., is that p and someone knows the fact, cause, result, then—though fact, cause, result cannot take wh-nominalisations—he knows that p, since if the fact, cause, result is that p, then it is the case that p.

A third subsidiary criterion used by Vendler rests on a confusion between a belief (suspicion, advice, etc.,) and what is believed (suspected, advised, etc.,). Though he rightly admits (p. 113) that, e.g., a statement that p can be subjective, while what is stated, namely that p, is objective, several of his arguments (e.g., pp. 106, 110–111) seem to rest on an assimilation either of the belief that p and what is believed when it is believed that p or of the *that p* which is the belief and the *that p* which is what is believed. Thus, it is assumed either that because the belief that p is subjective, then what is believed is subjective or that because the that p which is the belief is subjective, then the that p which is believed is subjective. But, in the first place, it does not follow from the fact that because when one believes that p, then one's belief is that p, or that when one suspects or fears that p, then one's suspicion or fear is that p, therefore the that p is the same in both cases. For, whereas to say that one's belief (suspicion, fear) is that p is to say that one's belief (suspicion, fear) is the belief (suspicion, fear) that p, to say one believes (suspects, fears) that p is not to say that one believes (suspects, fears) the belief (suspicion, fear) that p. The difference between the belief, suspicion, suggestion or advice that p and what is believed, etc., when it is believed, etc., that p can also be brought out in this way. To believe, suspect, suggest, advise, etc., that p is to believe in, suspect, advise X. Thus, to believe that fairies exist, to suspect that there has been foul play, to suggest that we have a swim, to advise that we return to work is to believe in fairies, to suspect foul play, to suggest a swim, to advise a return to work. Here the distinction is quite clear between the belief, suspicion, suggestion or advice and what is believed in, suspected, suggested or advised. Even though one can say both "A return to work is what I advise" and "A return to work is my advice," "I suggested a swim" and "My suggestion was a swim," it is clear that when my advice is a return to work or my suggestion is a swim, then my advice is the advice of a return to work and my suggestion is the suggestion of a swim. It is also quite clear that while the belief, suspicion, etc., may be "subjective," what is believed in, etc., is objective.

Hence, just as Vendler can rightly claim that, while one's statement can be true or false, what one states is not true or false, but can be so or not so, so equally it can be argued that, while one's suspicion or prediction can be correct or incorrect, what one suspects or predicts is not correct or incorrect, but something that can happen or something that can be too awful to contemplate.

It is a mistake to suppose that what someone believes is a belief, what he suspects is a suspicion or what he fears is a fear. That is, to put it in Aristotelian terms, it is a mistake to suppose, as does Vendler (p. 118), that the "immediate object" of believing is a belief, of suspecting a suspicion or of fearing a fear. Hence, one cannot argue, as he does, that what is believed is necessarily different from what is known on the ground that what is believed is a belief, whereas what is known is reality.

In a reply to two of his critics,[10] Vendler admits the earlier mentioned exceptions to his two main criteria and, therefore, adds a third criterion, namely, that it makes sense to qualify *subjective* verbs, but not *objective* verbs, by "falsely." Thus, one can believe, assume, predict falsely, but not know, tell, realise, remember, learn falsely, that p. In this way, Vendler can explain why, e.g., "suspect," "say," "predict" are used "subjectively" in suspect, say or predict that p, but "objectively" in suspect, say or predict, when, where or who. . . . One can wrongly suspect or incorrectly predict *that* so and so will happen; but to suspect or predict *where* or *when* it would happen—as contrasted with having (or voicing) a suspicion or making a prediction when or where it will happen—is to be right.

Now, though Vendler is undoubtedly correct in thinking that at least his last two main criteria mark off one group of verbs from another, neither he nor most of his critics seems to realise that what they show is (1) merely that the so called *subjective* verbs are

verbs such that to V that p does not imply that p, whereas the so
called *objective* verbs are verbs such that to V that p does imply
that p—and, of course, that to V where, when or how A F's does
imply that A F's in that place, time or manner in which it is Ved that
he does.[11] (2) that the so called *subjective* verbs—or, as Vendler in
his reply to two critics, Dunn and Suter, calls them, after Kiparsky
and Kiparsky, "non-factive" verbs—are the traditionally called
"intentional" verbs, and the so called *objective* verbs are the
traditionally called "non-intentional" verbs. It is, as is well
known, a characteristic of intentional verbs that they do not imply
that what is Ved need be so. This is why, e.g., whereas one can
suspect that p without its being the case that p, one cannot suspect
where X was without X's being where it was suspected to be. The
existence of three classes of verbs, namely those that can only be
intentional, e.g., believe, fear, hope or look for, those that can only
be non-intentional, e.g., know, realise, learn or find, and those that
can be sometimes one and sometimes the other, e.g., suspect,
predict or say, suggest that it is more accurate to speak of an
intentional or non-intentional use of a verb rather than of an
intentional or non-intentional verb, though I shall sometimes use
the latter terminology for stylistic reasons.

The important point to emphasise here is that from the fact that,
when a verb is used intentionally, to V that p does not imply that p,
whereas, when a verb is used non-intentionally, to V that p does
imply that p, it does not follow that the that p which is the object of
an intentionally used verb is different from the that p which is the
object of a non-intentionally used verb. Much less does it follow
that the object of the former is a proposition. To think the contrary
is simply to accept a hoary fallacy which it should not be necessary
to refute in this day and age. Yet, Vendler seems to assume that his
second and third criteria prove that the objects of *subjective* (=
intentional) verbs and the objects of *objective* (= non-intentional)
verbs are different and that the objects of the former are propositions. Perhaps his first criterion would help to show that at least the
objects of the two kinds of verbs are different, but, as we have
seen, the only evidence he produces for the truth of the first
criterion are dubious examples of what he considers to be bad
English, but which, his critics have rightly seen, are perfectly good

English. Moreover, he himself admits, indeed insists (p. 118), that, e.g., "the unbelievable is something utterly unlikely, unexpected or outrageous;" and these are not propositions, but something which could happen and could also be known. The same is true of unbelievable courage, stupidity or affrontery.

It is, therefore, worth showing very briefly—what I have argued at greater length elsewhere[12]—that there is no good reason for supposing that intentional verbs—Vendler's so called subjective verbs and Kiparsky's "non-factive" verbs—take objects different from non-intentional verbs; nor, *a fortiori,* that they take propositions as their objects. In so arguing I shall also be keeping my promise of the previous chapter to discuss the assumption that to believe that p is to believe the proposition that p, which we saw underlies the view of many philosophers that to know that p is to know the proposition that p.

What we believe when we believe that there are fairies at the bottom of the garden is what we see when we see that there are fairies there, just as what we diagnose when we diagnose that the patient has tuberculosis is what we discover when we discover that the patient has tuberculosis or as what we advise when we advise that there be a return to work is what happens when it happens that there is a return to work. And what we believe in when we believe in fairies is what we find when we find fairies just as what we diagnose when we diagnose tuberculosis is what we discover when we discover tuberculosis or as what we advise when we advise a return to work is what occurs when a return to work occurs. What we look for when we look for a vacant parking space is what we find when we find a vacant parking space. It is as absurd to say that someone who fears (expects, hopes, anticipates) that he will lose his money, fears (expects, hopes, anticipates) the proposition that he will lose his money as it would be to say that someone who fears (expects, hopes, anticipates) the loss of his money, fears (expects, hopes, anticipates) the concept of the loss of his money. Similarly, it is as absurd to say that someone who suspects that there has been foul play suspects the proposition that there has been foul play as it would be to say that someone who suspects foul play suspects the concept of foul play. Just as one would not be believing in, diagnosing or suspecting, what is not there if, *per impossibile,* what one believed in was the idea of fairies, what one diagnosed was the concept of tuberculosis or what one suspected was the thought of foul play, so one would not be believing, diagnosing, suspecting what is not so if what one believed was the proposition that there are fairies, or *per impossibile,* what one diagnosed was the proposition that the patient had tuberculosis or what one suspected was the proposition that foul play had been done. Yet one can undoubtedly diagnose, suspect or believe in, just as one can look for, what does not exist or diagnose, suspect or believe, just as one can hope for, what is not so. It is simply a mistake, however common a mistake, to argue that because one must believe, as one must diagnose, suspect, fear, expect or look for *something,* therefore there must exist some *thing,* e.g., a proposition or concept, which one believes, diagnoses, suspects, fears, expects or looks for. This is simply to misunderstand the force of the question "*What* do you believe, diagnose, suspect, fear, expect or look for?." It is, as we saw, to confuse a nominalisation-accusative with an object-accusative. But to believe that there are fairies or to believe in fairies is no more to be related to an object analogous to the object to which one is undoubtedly related when one believes a story or believes in a friend than to suspect that there has been foul play or to suspect foul play—or to advise that there be a return to work or to advise a return to work—is to be related to an object analogous to the object to which one is undoubtedly related when one suspects the butler—or advises a trade union. Such a confusion about belief and knowledge may, perhaps, have gained some of its plausibility from the fact that as well as believing (or knowing) that p one can, indeed, believe (or know) the proposition that p. By contrast, however, though one can suspect or advise that p, one cannot suspect or advise the proposition that p. Only someone as bold as Russell[13] could come out starkly with the assertion "It seems natural to say one believes a proposition and unnatural to say one desires a proposition, but as a matter of fact that is only a prejudice." Does Vendler really think that one anticipates, imagines, decides, predicts, suspects, promises or fears, hopes for, desires, diagnoses, advises, *propositions? What* we believe is not, contrary to what he says, a belief any more than what we predict is a prediction, what we suspect a suspicion or what we hope for a hope.

(III) KNOWING AND BELIEVING

Though Plato's arguments for denying any overlap at all between the possible objects of knowledge and belief and Vendler's arguments for denying an overlap between them when what one knows is that p and what one believes is that p are mistaken, it might be thought that there are two other categories of objects of knowledge which Vendler is right in thinking are not possible objects of belief. The first of these is the class of interrogatives and the second is a sub-class of the objects known by acquaintance.

(a) Interrogatives

Admittedly it makes no sense to use an interrogative after "believe" as it does after "know." We cannot believe, as we can know, either where, when, why, whom, what or how A V's or where, when, why, whom, what or how to V. A phrase like "Who (where) do you believe it was?" is only an apparent exception, because "believe" is here parenthetic and not really governing the wh-nominalisation. This is clear from the fact that we cannot say "Do you believe who (where) it was?." "Know" works in exactly the reverse way. We can say "Do you know who (where) it was?," but not "Who (where) do you know it was?." We also saw that, e.g., "believing what was said" is no exception to this rule that one cannot believe, though one can know, what something is, for the former uses the relative, not the interrogative, "what."

For the same reason one cannot believe, as one can know, the colour, size, weight, date, cause, result, etc., of something, since the nouns here really conceal interrogatives. Knowing the colour, size, etc., of something is knowing what the colour, size, etc., of something is; and this is not what we can believe. Further, since the noun or noun-phrase in, e.g., knowing French, *The Rime of the Ancient Mariner* or the twelve-times table also conceals an interrogative, e.g., how to speak, recite or calculate, we equally cannot speak of believing these things.

But, when one reduces, as we saw earlier one can, "knowing either what, whom, where, when or how to V or what, whom, where, when or how A V's" to its equivalent, namely "knowing that such and such is the thing, person, place, time or way either to V or which A V's," one can then co-ordinate it with a matching "believing that such and such is the thing, person, place, time or way to V or which A V's." Similarly, one can reduce "knowing the colour, weight, etc.," to "knowing what the colour, weight, etc., is" and, thence, to "knowing that the colour, weight, etc., is so and so" and match the latter with "believing that the colour, weight, etc., is so and so." One can also reduce "knowing one's twelve times table" to "knowing for each number from one to twelve, that the product of it and either itself or each other number from one to twelve is so and so" and then match the latter with "believing, for each number from one to twelve, that the product of it and either itself or each other number from one to twelve is so and so."

Given, as Vendler would allow, that underlying each wh-nominalisation there is a that-nominalisation, the question whether one can believe what one knows either when one knows what, whom, where, when or how to V or what, whom, where, when or how A V's or when one knows, e.g., one's twelve times table, despite the fact that "believe" cannot be followed by a wh-nominalisation or by their equivalent nouns, such as "colour," "weight," "twelve times tables," reduces to the original question whether what one believes when one believes that p is the same as what one knows when one knows that p. And to this question I have already argued that the answer is "Yes."

Incidentally, one can also either know or believe X to be Y, e.g., know or believe a man to be hardworking, a gearbox to be faulty or a proposition to be true or false. We saw, however, that knowing or believing X to be Y is only a variation on knowing or believing that X is Y and must, therefore, be treated in the same way as the latter.

(b) Acquaintance

Among objects known by acquaintance, we can distinguish between those which clearly cannot be both known and believed and those which *prima facie* can. It obviously makes no sense to talk of believing, as it does of knowing, a town, a building, an author's works, pain, poverty, a voice or a face. On the other hand, one can either know or believe a person or his story, though one can know him or it without believing him or it and, conversely, believe him or it without knowing him or it. There are a few politicians whom I believe, though I do not personally know them, and many whom I do know but do not believe.

But the class of objects known by acquaintance, whether or not it includes some which can also be believed, is irrelevant to our problem, viz., whether *what* is known and believed can be the same. For, as I have argued earlier, these objects are not *what* we know; they are not "objects of knowledge" in the sense in which our knowledge is composed of what we know. Knowing them is not like knowing dates, causes, times or colours or knowing where or when or how or that. There is no question here of our belief changing to knowledge or of being implied or not implied by knowledge or of our having good reason to believe but not being in a position to know or of contrasting the weak position of those who only believe them with the strong position of those who know them.

Conversely, the people or stories we believe are equally not "objects of belief" in the same way that either that p or the fairies and cold baths we believe in are objects of belief. The former are what our beliefs are directed to; the latter what they consist in.

(c) That p

Except for Plato and Vendler, almost all philosophers, including Plato himself in, e.g., the *Meno* and *Theaetetus*, have gone further and held, indeed, that when what is known is that p and what is believed is that p, these are the same. This view has, however, never really been argued for, but has simply been based on the assumption that the same thing which is believed and known when we believe and know that p is the *proposition that p*. Moreover, we have seen that Plato and Vendler's contrary thesis was based on the explicity argued for premise that what is believed is a proposition (an appearance, according to Plato), while what is known is something other than a proposition, e.g., a fact (a Form, according to Plato).

On the contrary, I argued, in section B(ii) of this chapter, against the assumption, common to both sides in the dispute, that what is believed when one believes that p is the proposition that p and, in section F of the previous chapter, against the assumption made by most philosophers, but disputed by Vendler (and perhaps by Plato in the *Republic*), that what is known when one knows that p is the proposition that p. We saw that "that p" is not an "object" of knowledge or belief in the sense that somebody known by acquaintance is an actual "object" of knowledge and a possible "object" of belief and something known by acquaintance is an actual object of knowledge. The that-nominalisation—or its equivalent noun-phrase—is used to answer the question "What is known or believed?" in such a way as to characterise the nature of the knowledge or belief itself just as the nature of advice given or of a question asked is revealed by the that-nominalisation or noun-phrase which answers "What is being advised or asked?." More importantly for our present purpose, there is no reason to suppose that *what is Ved* is a different kind of thing for different instances of "Ving," though whether or not what is Ved must exist or be so does depend on the nature of V. Thus, as we have seen, what is discovered is the same as what is suspected when foul play—or that there has been foul play—is suspected and discovered, though one can suspect, but not discover, foul play when there is none; and what is divulged is the same as what is suggested when what is suggested and divulged is a new name for a ship, even though one can suggest, but not divulge, a new name that will not be assigned. Similarly, what is known and what is believed when what is known and believed is that Napoleon lost the Battle of Waterloo is the same even though one cannot know, as one can believe, what is not so.

It is important to stress here that so far all I have been discussing is the question whether what is believed and what is known *can* be the same. This is quite a different question both from the implausible and never, as far as I know, argued for, question whether believing something implies knowing it and from the question, very commonly answered in the affirmative, whether knowing something implies believing it. Yet, philosophers have often confused the question already discussed with this latter question. Thus, those (e.g., Ayer) who argue that to know that p implies to believe that p assume that it is the same sort of thing which is known and believed, whereas those (e.g., Vendler)[14] who argue that the same sort of thing cannot be believed and known assume

that this disproves that one can analyse knowing that p in terms of
believing that p. But those few philosophers, including myself,
who deny that knowing that p implies believing that p have, quite
consistently, held that the *that p* which can be known and believed
is the same, whether, like the majority, they have supposed that
this common "that p" expresses a proposition or, like myself, that
it does not. What has been confused is the question whether what
can be known is a segment of what can be believed and the
question whether what *is* known is and must be a segment of what
is believed. On the former assumption knowing something would
imply that one can believe it; on the latter that one does believe it. I
shall discuss the question whether knowing something implies
actually believing it in the next chapter, since it is a traditionally
subscribed-to test of knowledge.

C. DIFFERENTIAE OF THE KNOWN

In the previous chapter we saw that whatever is an "object" of
knowledge, in the philosophical sense as contrasted with the ordinary sense in which only what is known by acquaintance is an
"object" of knowledge, is really some kind of instance of what is
known when it is known *that p*. Thus, to know where, what, how,
etc., A V's or where, what, how to V, to know X to be Y, to know
the colour, etc., of something or to know Greek is to know that. We
have, earlier in this chapter, agreed that the areas of knowledge
and belief can overlap when what is known is that p. An important
task, therefore, is to examine the criteria by which the areas of
what can be known and what can be believed have been marked
off. There have been at least three of these; that what is known
must be true, that it must be necessary and that it must be certain.
Let us consider each of these in turn.

(i) TRUTH

Traditionally the prime condition of something's being capable of
being known has been that it be true.[15] What is undoubtedly correct
in this view is this: If it is true to say that something is known, then

it must also be true to say that what is known is so, whereas it can be true to say that something is believed without its being true to say that what is believed is so. To this it might be objected, first, that such a version is straightforwardly applicable only to "knowing that p," for it is here that the notion of truth most plausibly gets a foothold, as when we say that if someone knows that the earth goes round the sun, then it must be true that the earth goes round the sun. If, however, "knowing where, when, what, how" either with an indicative, infinitive or modal can, as I argued in an earlier chapter, be counted as variations on "knowing that"—so that someone who knows where the buried treasure is knows that it is in that place in which it in fact is and someone who knows how to play chess knows that the way to play it is the way which is in fact the way to play it—then the notion of truth can with equal plausibility enter into knowledge of these things.

Secondly, even where plausible, the traditional view that truth is a necessary criterion of knowledge is misleading, for when one knows, e.g., that the earth goes round the sun, what is known, namely that the earth goes round the sun, is the case. What is true is the statement expressing what is the case, namely that the earth goes round the sun. In other words, to know that p implies that p, and it is only because "p" implies "It is true that p" that, therefore, to know that p implies that it is true that p. Similarly, if it is known that a statement is true, what follows immediately is that the statement is true and it only secondarily follows that it is true that the statement is true. It is usually because philosophers[16] implicitly collapse into one the two steps "to know that p implies p" and "p implies p is true" or move from "If A knows that p, then p" to "If it is true that A knows that p, then it is true that p," that they take truth, rather than reality, as a necessary condition of knowledge. Similarly, "A knows how to spell 'deceive' " primarily implies that the way to spell "deceive" is the way he could offer and, only secondarily, that it is true that this is the way to spell it. Sometimes,[17] however, the criterion that what is known must be true is based on the supposition that when someone knows that p, "p" stands for the proposition p, that is, something which can be true or false. But we saw earlier that it is a false supposition that what is known when it is known that p—or what is believed, suspected, feared, when it is believed, suspected, feared that p—is the proposition p.

It should be noticed that none of this shows either that knowing something implies knowing that the statement expressing it is true—which would be incorrect for animals and for humans who did not realise that a particular "q" expresses p—or that knowing that a statement is true implies knowing that which the statement expresses—for one might not know what a statement known to be true in fact stated.

It is, therefore, preferable to state this condition, not in terms of what is known being true, but in terms of its being so and, hence, to speak of reality rather than truth as the prime condition for knowledge. Many philosophers, indeed, hop about unwittingly between talking of what is known being true and of what is known being so. Furthermore, Plato's insistence that knowledge can be only of what is and Vendler's view that it is of reality are natural variations on the view I am suggesting.

In knowledge by acquaintance of people, places or conditions, such as pain, poverty or an unhappy childhood, reality has the same primary place and truth the same secondary place as in the rest of knowledge, since, as we saw earlier, what is known here, that is the content of knowledge, is the same as in the rest of knowledge. Moreover, the reality, unlike the truth, of the object known, whether persons, place or condition, is a necessary condition for knowledge, since one cannot know some person or place which does not exist or have known a condition which one has never experienced. Indeed, one can only know these while they exist.

Taken, therefore, in the broadest way, so as to cover not only the possession of information, of answers to questions, including the way to do things, and of acquaintance with persons, things and conditions, the reality of what is known is a *necessary* condition for knowledge of it.

It needs no argument to show that neither reality nor truth is a *sufficient* condition for knowledge, since clearly, as Aristotle emphasised,[19] something could be either real or true without being known to be so. It may well be that Homer lived in Greece in 900 BC and wrote both the *Iliad* and the *Odyssey*, though no one knows that he did and, therefore, does not know when or where he lived and what he wrote or who he was. He could have lived an isolated existence unknown to anyone. And there could be a way to sing his verses, though no one knows how to do it.

(II) NECESSITY

Many philosophers have narrowed the area of the known from what must be true (or what must be so) to what must be necessarily true (or necessarily so).

Thus, in the *Republic* Plato insisted that what can be known is confined not merely to what *is* but to what is *unchanging* in contrast to what can be believed, which is something which can shift between what is and what is not. Whereas, he argued, something which is small, black or good can become big, white or bad, smallness, blackness or goodness themselves cannot ever be other than they are. Hence, he concluded, one can only believe, rightly or wrongly, that something is small, black or good, but one can attain to knowledge of smallness, blackness or goodness as one can to knowledge of beauty and truth.

Aristotle, in his *Posterior Analytics,*[20] gave qualified support to Plato's view that the areas of the knowable and of the believable are distinct by delineating that of the former as what is necessary or cannot be otherwise and that of the latter as what is contingent or can be otherwise.

This view has come down to us chiefly in the form in which it was advocated by Hume and, in slightly different language, by the Logical Positivists. In his *Treatise*[21] of 1738, Hume argued that the objects of both knowledge and belief are relations between ideas. Some of these relations, he held, depend solely on the ideas which they relate and cannot, therefore, change without a change in these ideas. For example, the relation of equality between the sum of the angles of a triangle and two right angles is invariable because it holds in virtue of the idea of a triangle. The angles of a (Euclidean) triangle are necessarily equal to two right angles. Only such relations, he held, can be the objects of knowledge; though they can also be the objects of belief. We can know—or believe—that the angles of a triangle add up to two right angles. By contrast, there are relations which may be present or absent even while the ideas they relate remain the same. Thus, though in fact a triangle is an uncommon shape for a room, this is not something that could not be altered without altering the idea of a triangle. Such relations, Hume held, can only be the objects of belief and not of knowledge. In a later work, the *Inquiry Concerning Human Understanding*[22] of 1748, he described this division as a division of the "objects of human reason or inquiry" into "Relations of ideas" and "Matters of fact." He still contrasted them as those things whose contrary is not possible and would imply a contradiction and those things whose contrary is possible and would not imply a contradiction. And he confined knowledge to the former group.

The Logical Positivists usually explicitly acknowledged[23] Hume as the source of their view that only what is necessarily true can be known and that anything else can only be believed. Hence, they were led to deny that we can know any but a tiny area of what we commonly think we know. We cannot, on this view, know that London is in the south of England, that there are more motor cars on the road than there were 100 years ago or that the sun will rise tomorrow. Furthermore, their basic reason for this view is exactly the same as Hume's, namely, that nothing can be known if there is a *possibility* of its not being so or of its being false. However varied the arguments for their thesis, this reason underlies them all.

Sometimes what is emphasised is the possibility of a particular true statement's not being true. Hence, it is held that no empirical statement, e.g., that Napoleon lost the Battle of Waterloo, can be known to be true, since an empirical statement is a statement the truth of whose opposite is possible.[24] Sometimes what is emphasised is the possibility of a particular argument's not proving its conclusion.[25] It is pointed out that an argument for a conclusion typical of science and everyday life, as contrasted with an argument for a conclusion typical of mathematics and logic, is such that, even though its premises are both true and known to be true, yet it is logically possible for its conclusion to be false. This is, indeed, what is meant by calling it a non-deductive argument. Thus, though we can say, in logic, that if Socrates is a man and all men are mortal, it follows that Socrates is mortal, we cannot say that, however great the evidence one has for thinking that James

Joyce wrote *Finnegans Wake* and however many future tests would confirm this, it follows that James Joyce did write *Finnegans Wake*.

Sometimes what is emphasised is the possibility of a particular piece of evidence's being otherwise than is required. For instance, it is said that, though for the sake of argument, the above piece of reasoning allowed that one could know that however many tests were carried out they would all point to the same conclusion, in fact this cannot be known. For, since the series of tests is infinite, the possibility of one of them's not supporting the conclusion cannot be ruled out.[27] We need not discuss the assertion that the series of such tests must be infinite, but only underline that the reasoning again uses the assumption that something cannot be known if its opposite is possible.

Sometimes, we are reminded how often and how easily we are deceived when we move to a conclusion.[28] We are taken in by illusions, suffer from hallucinations, are misled by perspectives, confuse dreams with waking life and make miscalculations. Is there not always the possibility in a given case of some such mistake? And if this is possible, then one cannot, it is said, know that it is not so. Many philosophers—from Aristotle through Aquinas to the present day—have been so convinced what is known must be necessary that they have supposed either that the future, because it is contingent, cannot be known, or that, since an omniscient God always does know the future, it must be determined and, thus, incompatible with free-will.

We must, therefore, ask why it should seem so obvious, as it has to many philosophers, that something cannot be known to be so if there is the possibility of its not being so. The answer, I think, is that it is easy to get confused about modal concepts, such as those expressed by "can," "must" and "possible."

We have already seen that knowledge is such that one cannot know what is not so (or what is false) or, as we can also put it, that what is known to be so (or true) must be so (or true) or that what is known is necessarily so (or true). The correct way to read this is as "It cannot be that what is known is not so (or is false)" or as "It must be that what is known is so (is true);" that is, the possibility of anything's being both known and not so (or false) is ruled out. In symbols ~M (Kp.p̄). But it is easy to read the original wrongly as "What is known is the sort of thing that cannot be not so (or false)" or as "What is known is the sort of thing that must be so (or true);" that is, something's being known and the possibility of that thing's being not so (or false) is ruled out. In symbols ~ (Kp.Mp̄) (or ~ M(Kp.Mp̄). What has happened is that the false thesis has wrongly transferred the modal "must" or "cannot" from the combination of the two items to the second item.

This is clear also from another way of putting the point. It is easy to confuse the correct statement that "If A knows that X is Y, then necessarily (i.e., it follows that) it is true that X is Y" and the incorrect statement that "If A knows that X is Y, then X is Y is necessarily true (i.e., "X is Y" is a necessarily true statement)." Indeed, because we can logically only know what is so (or true), then the compound statement "If A knows that X is Y, then X is Y" is necessarily true, whether the sub-statement "X is Y" is itself a necessarily true statement, such as "A triangle has three sides," or a contingently true statement, such as "Napoleon lost the Battle of Waterloo." The necessity of the compound statement does not imply the necessity of either of its parts. To say correctly that we can only know what is so (or true) is not to say, as do the philosophers we are discussing, that we can only know what is necessarily so (or true). It is what *is* not so (or is false), not what *can* be not so (or can be false), that cannot be known.

In case it may seem almost incredible that philosophers should have based a thesis about what can be known on a mere modal mistake, it is worth pointing out that a similar, and perhaps even grosser, instance, namely that of supposing that what *is* so, *must* be so and *cannot not* be so, has often led philosophers, from Aristotle onwards,[29] to adopt some form of determinism. They have taken the principle that something which is so could not be not so incorrectly to read that things must be as they are instead of correctly to read that nothing can both be so and not be so. To say that it cannot be that something is so and is not so is not to say that it cannot be that something is so and could be not so.

Something's being so or being true is in no way incompatible with the possibility of its not being so or not being true. If something is so or is true, then it can be known. There is no good reason for supposing that the mere possibility of its not being so or not being true makes it incapable of being known.

(III) CERTAINTY

Many philosophers, including Hume and the Logical Positivists,[30] have failed to distinguish clearly between the possibility *for* something not *to be so* or not to be true and the possibility *that* it *is* not so or is not true. Hence, they have assimilated the view that the former possibility precludes knowledge and the view that the latter possibility precludes it. Since the former possibility is the opposite of *necessity*, while the latter is the opposite of *certainty*, they have oscillated between the view that only what is necessary can be known and the view that only what is certain can be known. Thus, Hume is followed by the Logical Positivists in contrasting the area of knowledge and the area of belief in two different ways, namely that of the necessary with the contingent and that of the certain with the probable and, indeed, frequently getting mixed up with a cross-divisional contrast between the necessary and the probable. Even a casual glance at the writings of these philosophers shows that, having proved—what is not really in dispute—that no contingent matter is necessary because there is always a possibility of its being other than it is, they argued that the existence of the possibility of its being other than it is shows that there is no certainty in the matter and, because there is no certainty, there is no knowledge.

The objections to all this are threefold. First, the possibility which is contrasted with necessity is not the same as that which is contrasted with certainty. Secondly, the existence of the former possibility of something's being other than it is does not exclude knowledge of its being as it is. Thirdly, the existence of the latter possibility does not exclude knowledge of its being as it is, though it does exclude, what we shall see is quite different, both any certainty and any knowing for certain that it is as it is. Since we have just discussed the second objection, we need examine only the other two.

(1) The possibility which is contrasted with necessity is quite different from that which is contrasted with certainty.[31] The former is commonly expressed in English either with an accusative and

infinitive construction—possible for A to V—or with a that-nominalisation in the subjunctive mood—possible that A (should) V. It is possible for a triangle to have all its sides equal or possible that it (should) have all its sides equal. The latter possibility is commonly expressed in English by a that-nominalisation in the indicative mood. It is possible that a triangle was a sacred symbol among certain secret societies in the Middle Ages. The former possibility is also expressed in English by the modal "can"—a triangle can have all its sides equal—while the latter possibility is expressed by "may"—a triangle may have been a sacred symbol among certain secret societies in the Middle Ages. The former possibility, like its opposite necessity, can be qualified as logical, physical, practical, legal, economic, financial, etc.; but these qualifications do not go with the latter possibility and its opposite certainty.

Most importantly for our present purpose, the possibility which excludes necessity is implied by, but does not imply, the possibility which excludes certainty. Thus, if it is possible that I saw the numberplate at 50 yards, it must be possible for me to have seen it at that distance; but it could be possible for me to have seen the numberplate at 50 yards without its being possible that I did see it. Hence, any proof that only what cannot be otherwise—that is, only what is necessary—can be known would also be a proof that only what may not be otherwise—that is, only what is certain—can be known; but a proof that only what may not be otherwise—and is, therefore, certain—can be known would not necessarily be a proof that only what cannot be otherwise—and is, therefore, necessary—can be known. On the other hand, a disproof of the thesis that only what is necessary can be known is not in itself a disproof of the thesis that only what is certain can be known. Nevertheless, this latter thesis can be shown to be as mistaken as the former.

(2) First, this thesis has usually been based on a confusion parallel to—though not, as was wrongly thought, identical with—that underlying the previously discussed thesis, that if something is known, then it is not possible for it to be otherwise than it is known to be. This confusion, on analogy with its parallel, is between the incorrect view that if something is known to be so, it is not possible that it is not so and the correct view, that it is not possible that

something is known to be so and is not so. Like the other, it is a case of a misplaced modal.

Secondly, and perhaps more importantly in the history of philosophy, there has been a general tendency[32] to equate knowledge and certainty either in the form that knowing something is the same as being certain about it or in the quite different form that what is known is the same as what is certain.[33] Though I shall try to show that both these theses are mistaken, it is the latter which is our immediate problem. The former will be examined in the next chapter.

Any equation of what is known with what is certain must be wrong, for what is certain need not be known. It could well be certain that the earth will be desolated by solar radiation before AD 2000, although no-one knows or even thinks this. The circumstances which make something certain need not make it known. Even for the past, the evidence which excludes, by revealing the non-existence of, the possibility that something is not so, and hence makes it certain that it is so, need not be appreciated as such by those who have this evidence. Furthermore, if whatever was certainly so was known to be so, then whatever was necessarily so would also have to be known to be so, since whatever is necessarily so is certainly so. But there can be many necessary results which are not known.

The view, expressed by G. E. Moore,[34] that "a thing can't be certain unless it is known" depends—as he later partly saw[35]—on assimilating this mistaken view to the plausible view that no-one would, or could appropriately, *say* that something was certain unless he thought, and was therefore prepared to assert, that he, or somebody, knew it.

Similarly, though, "The possibility that not-p is not excluded" follows from "It is not certain that p", it does not, as Moore thought,[35] follow from, much less is it logically or in meaning equivalent to, "Nobody knows (or knows for certain) that p". It is because Moore thought that what is certain is relative to somebody's knowledge that he also, wrongly, held[35] that "Two different people who say at the same time about the same proposition p, the one 'It is certain (or 'possible', as he says in another passage) that p is true', the other 'It is not certain (or 'possible') that p is true', may both be saying what is true and not contradicting one another".

Since the mistaken thesis that if something is certain it must be known is equivalent to the thesis that if it is not known, it is not certain and, therefore, the possibility of its opposite is not excluded, to say that if it is not known that p, then it is possible that not-p is also mistaken. Equally mistaken is a recent variation[38] on this view, according to which "a state of affairs is possible if it is not known not to obtain, and no practicable investigations would establish that it does not obtain." If this were correct, it would follow, by contraposition, that if this state of affairs is not possible then either it is known that or practicable investigations would establish that it does not obtain. But there is no reason at all to suppose that nothing can be certain unless practicable investigations would establish the non-existence of its opposite. Such a view borrows part of its plausibility from the fact that a reason for supposing something to be certain is a supposition that its opposite can be practically disproved and partly from the fact that if something is certain, then its opposite does not exist.

Having established that what is certain need not be known, let us enquire whether what is known need be certain.

First, this view may rely on the argument that because it is certain that, if it is known that p, then p—which itself follows from the fact that it is necessarily true that, if it is known that p, then p—therefore, if it is known that p, it is certain that p. But the principle underlying this argument, namely, that if it is certain that if p, then q, then if p, it is certain that q, is as mistaken as the analogous principle that if it is necessarily true that if p, then q, then if p, it is necessarily true that q. For, according to it, from the correct premise that it is certain (because necessary) that if p, then p, there would follow the mistaken conclusion that if p, then it is certain that p. What both arguments do is to argue from the necessity or certainty of the connexion between p and q to the necessity or certainty of q itself; that is from "It is certain (necessary) that it follows" or "It certainly (necessarily) follows" to "It follows that it is certain (necessary)." "If p, then certainly q" no more means "If p, it is certain that q" than "If p, then obviously, clearly, evidently, probably q," means "If p, it is obvious, clear, evident, probable that q." For if they did, the contrapositives would be "If it's not certain, obvious, clear, evident, probable that q, then not-p;" but the actual contrapositives are "If not-q, then certainly, obviously, clearly, probably, evidently not-*p*." Hence, the fact that it is certain that if it is known that *p*, then *p* no more provides a reason for supposing that if it is known that *p*, then it is certain that *p* than the fact that it is necessary that if it is known that *p*, then *p* provides a reason for supposing that if it is known that *p*, then it is necessary that *p*.

Secondly, the view that what is known must be certain may depend on wrongly assuming that, because some ways in which I come to know something are such that I thereby make certain of it, therefore, whenever and however I come to know something, I thereby make certain of it and so reveal that it is certain. But this is to confuse *know* and *know for certain*.[39] It is true that if something is known for certain, then it is certain, for to know for certain is to know in such a way that the possibility that what is known to be so might be other than it is, is excluded. But it does not follow that because its being known for certain that *p* implies that it is certain that *p*, therefore its being known that *p* implies that it is certain that *p*.

Thirdly, this view, beloved of sceptical philosophers,[40] limits the area of knowledge in a quite implausible way. People often claim, and rightly, to know things which are not certain. Furthermore, if what is correctly believed can, without further change in it, become known, then, on the assumption under discussion, only what is certain could be correctly believed. And this is false.

Finally, if whatever is known is therefore certain, the interesting, and perhaps awkward, consequence follows that if there is anything which cannot be so without being known to be so, then it is also something which cannot be so without being certain. In other words, it is something for which the generally invalid inference "*p* implies it is certain that *p*"[41] would be valid. For instance, if a man in full possession of his senses cannot help knowing that he is alive and knowing whether and what he is feeling and thinking, then if he is alive and feeling and thinking so-and-so, it is certain that he is. And if God knows all, then all is certain.

G. E. Moore[42] on one occasion tried to avoid this conclusion by arguing that for the truth of "It is certain that *p*" "I know that *p*" is sufficient, but not necessary, while "Somebody knows that *p*" is necessary, but not sufficient. Thus, on the one hand, Hitler's knowledge that he is alive would not show that he is certainly alive, but mine would; while, on the other, for it to be certain that he is dead requires somebody's knowledge of it, though not mine. This attempt to escape from his own dilemma will not, however, work. The second alternative implies the conclusion, which we have already seen to be false, that what is certain must be known; while the first alternative commits us to the debatable conclusion that by knowing that p I make it certain that p.

I conclude, therefore, that it is a mistake to suppose that only what is certain, that is only that which it is not possible that it is otherwise, can be known.

We have now discussed the three main restrictions which philosophers have commonly, at one time or other, put on the extent of our knowledge, namely that of truth, necessity and certainty; and have rejected the latter two entirely and the former in the narrow way in which it has sometimes been interpreted. There are, of course, further quite different ways in which the extent of our knowledge has been confined, but these all depend on assumptions about the nature of the world or about the methods by which knowledge about it would have to be sought.[43] Thus, just as Plato disallowed any knowledge of the world we live in because he held that such a world, in contrast with that other in which the pure Forms of Beauty, Truth, Number, etc., abide, is only illusory, so a long line of philosophers from Descartes, through Locke, Berkeley and Hume, to Mill and many early 20th century philosophers have held that knowledge is restricted to what they called, in the 17th and 18th centuries, "ideas" and, in the 20th century, "sense-data." Again, sceptical philosophers have varied from those who held that no matters of fact at all can be known because none is certain to those who held, e.g., that nothing can be known about the future because knowledge is confined to what exists or has existed and the future does not, or that no one can know anything about the feelings and thoughts of others because such knowledge, like knowledge of one's own thoughts and feelings, would only be possible for someone who had these thoughts and feelings. But since these restrictions on the extent of our knowledge are due more to the alleged nature of the candidates for knowledge than to the notion of knowledge itself, I shall not discuss them here.

CHAPTER FOUR

Criteria of Knowledge

We saw in the first chapter that the fact that someone knows something does not imply that someone, whether himself or another, claims to know it or even that he could justify such a claim if it were made or that he can prove that he knows it. We can, therefore, distinguish between a criterion or condition of knowledge and a test of any claim to it. Nevertheless, those factors which constitute the criteria or conditions necessary and sufficient for something to be knowledge can be both tests of whether someone knows it and ways to verify any claim that he knows it. Whether we are interested in these factors as criteria, conditions or tests, we can regard an enquiry into them as asking what does the knowledge of something imply and what is it implied by.

The criteria for knowing something could, in principle, be different either if what it is to know one sort of thing were different from what it is to know another sort—as, perhaps, practising the piano is different from practising law—or if, though "know" does not signify different ideas, a difference in the objects known entailed a difference in the implications of knowing them—as when suspecting the butler implies, whereas suspecting foul play does not, that what is suspected exists. Thus, for either of these reasons, knowing a person might imply, whereas knowing who he is might not, that one has met him.

As a matter of historical fact, philosophers[1] since the time of Plato's *Theaetetus*—and certainly in the present century—have usually concentrated on the criteria or conditions for the knowledge which is expressed in English as "knowing that p," e.g., that the Battle of Waterloo was fought in 1815 or that the earth goes round the sun. Since I argued earlier that the other grammatical forms in which knowledge is expressed, e.g., knowing what or where to V or what or where A V's, knowing the size of X, etc., are logically variations on "knowing that," we can follow this traditional path, though with an explicit caution where the grammatical variations may affect the criteria.

In the previous chapter we considered the extent of our knowledge and, hence, the conditions for what is known being the sort of thing which could be known, e.g., that it is so (or true), that it is necessary or that it is certain. Here I want to examine the criteria for someone's knowing any of those things which can be known. Clearly the question what sorts of things can be known and the question what knowledge of them is are different, though connected, for something could be so, necessary and/or certain—and, hence, the sort of thing which on the previous (debatable) criteria could be known—though it is not in fact known. There is, no doubt, a multitude of things which are so, which are necessary and which are certain, but which no one yet knows or may ever know. On the other hand, of course, no one could know any of those things which for one or other reason cannot be known.

Throughout the history of past and present philosophy various criteria of knowledge have been offered, though the traditional lists[2] have usually not distinguished between the conditions for what is known and the criteria for knowing it. Such lists include the ideas of being right—often assimilated to the idea of being true—of believing and/or of being certain, of being justified and of having used a certain method or having been led along a certain route. I shall examine each of these criteria in turn.

A. RIGHT.

The prime criterion for knowledge is being right. That is, one cannot know and yet be wrong. This is the opposite side of the coin to the condition that what is known must be (or be true). No one could know that the sun goes round the earth if he is incorrect about its direction, know where the buried treasure is if it is not in the place he thinks it is, know how to solve an equation if he cannot do it in the right way, know a person he has not met, or have known pain and poverty of which he has never been conscious. One could, of course, say or think that something was known when in fact one was wrong, as, e.g., it was once said to be known that the sun goes round the earth. And one might, indeed, be justified in saying or thinking this, if one had good reasons for doing so. But it would not follow that what one had good reasons for thinking or saying one was correct in thinking or saying, much less, therefore, that one knew this. It makes sense to say that someone mistakenly or erroneously believes so and so, but not that he mistakenly or erroneously knows it. And this is a characteristic of the concept of *knowledge*, not a "relatively trivial linguistic necessity" of the English word "know."[3]

Though to know implies to be right, we shall see that it no more implies to know or think that one is right than it implies to know, or think, that one knows. Nor does it imply actually manifesting one's correctness either in word or deed. On the other hand, being right does not imply knowing. There are, as we shall see, many reasons, such as luck, chance, coincidence, guesswork, mutually cancelling mistakes, etc., why being right does not show that one knows. Being right is a necessary, but not a sufficient, criterion of knowledge, even though in many situations it may be mistaken for knowledge and may often, as Plato emphasised, serve the same purpose.

B. CERTAINTY

A second criterion commonly offered for knowledge is that of certainty. We saw in the previous chapter that knowledge and certainty have in the history of philosophy frequently been equated both in the form that what is known and what is certain are the same and in the form that knowing something and being certain of it are the same. Having there argued against the former equation, let us now examine the latter.

Any equation of *knowing* that p and *being certain* that p must be mistaken, for the one neither implies nor is implied by the other. A man can be (or feel) certain that p without knowing that p, still more without knowing that he knows that p[5] and, indeed, even without being right in supposing that p. One man can be certain that p and another be certain of the opposite, but if somebody knows that p, no-one can know the opposite. Contrariwise, a man can know that p without being (or feeling) certain that p[6] and without thinking or feeling that p is certain, though not without being right in supposing that p. There can well be many things which I know though I am not certain of them, for I do not have to think that there is no possibility that I am wrong in order to know something. Indeed I may well know something without either knowing or even thinking that I do know it.

The notions of *knowing* that p and *being certain* that p are, indeed, quite different. Knowing, unlike being certain, implies being right. One can sound or look certain, but there is no physical expression of knowledge. Certainty, but not knowledge, is something one can feel, something one can induce in oneself or another, something one can discover in oneself introspectively or in another behaviouristically. We can ask *how* somebody knows that p, but not how he is certain that p; and, conversely, *why* he is certain, but not why he knows. To ask how certain he is is quite different from asking how he is certain and also from how knowledgeable he is. One can argue that if somebody knows that p, then it is known that p, but not that if somebody is certain that p, then it is certain that p.

One source of the confusion[7] about *knowing* and *being certain* may lie in the fact that one commonly, though not necessarily, says "I know" when one is certain and *vice-versa*. But the appropriateness of saying "I know" must not be confused with its truth. And, as we have just seen, there is no implication between *knowing* and *being certain*. A second source of the confusion may spring from the connexion between knowing or not knowing what to do and being certain or uncertain about one's plans or intentions. Not knowing what to call one's dog is the result of indecision or uncertainty; all that one needs for knowledge here, unlike knowing what one's neighbour's dog is called, is to make up one's mind. But it is the end of the uncertainty that gives us the knowledge, and not *vice-versa*. Contrariwise, a third source of the assimilation of the two notions may be that coming to know something can, though it need not, end one's uncertainty about it, whether what one comes to know is what to do or what is the case.

A fourth source of the confusion between somebody's knowing and being certain and possibly also of that between something's being known and being certain is the assimilation of *knowing* or of *being certain* to *knowing for certain*.[8] But, in fact, "know for certain" is neither a redundant form of "know" nor an equivalent of "be certain" nor a conjunction of the two.

"Knowing for certain" cannot be the same as "knowing and being certain," since "for certain" here means, as it does also in "tell, establish, show, discover for certain" that something is certain, whereas "being certain" here means only that somebody is certain. One could know and be certain that p even though one did not know for certain that p. Yet, although "for certain" implies that something rather than someone is certain, "know (can tell, establish) for certain" does not mean[9] that it is certain that someone knows (can tell, establish), that is, that someone certainly knows (can tell, establish), but that someone knows (can tell, establish) in such a way that what is known (told, established) is revealed as certain.

Nor can *knowing for certain* be the same as *being certain*. *Knowing for certain* implies *knowing* and, therefore, being right, whereas we have seen already that one can be certain without knowing or even being right and also know without being certain.

Nor, finally, can *knowing for certain* be the same as simply *knowing*, because, although the former implies the latter, it is not implied by it. To know for certain, like to tell, establish, discover, make out for certain, is to know in such a way that the possibility that one is mistaken is excluded. If, on the other hand, one simply knows, then though it follows that one *is not* mistaken, it does not follow that *it is not possible* that one is mistaken.[10] A failure to distinguish these two is easy if in the former one replaces "follows" by "cannot be that not," thus giving the correct assertion "If one knows, it cannot be that one is not right." But a similar replacement in the latter form then gives us the quite different and incorrect assertion "If one knows, it cannot be that it is possible that one is not right." Even if, what I disputed above, "It is known that p" implies that it is certain that p, it cannot be concluded that "It is known that p" implies that it is known for certain that p; for "It is certain that p," as we saw, does not imply that it is known that p, much less that is is known for certain that p. If it is certain that p, then there must exist circumstances which either make it certain that p or would show that it is certain that p, but someone who knows that p need not know of the existence nor appreciate the force of these circumstances; and, therefore, need not know for certain that p.

We see, therefore, that somebody's knowing that p and somebody's being certain that p are so far from being the same that neither implies the other.

C. BELIEF

A third criterion of knowledge commonly suggested from Plato's day to the present is that of belief.

Clearly, no one would argue that belief is *sufficient* for knowledge, either in the form that believing something implies knowing it or in the form that believing that one knows something implies that one does know it. One can believe, but not know, what is not so or not true; whereas we saw in the previous chapter that what is known must be so—or, in the misleading traditional version, must be true. That the sun goes round the earth was once as firmly and as widely believed as it is now believed that the earth goes round the sun, but only the latter could ever be known, for only the latter is so. We have just shown that while erroneous, incorrect or false belief is all too common, erroneous, incorrect or false knowlege is an absurdity. Equally, it is because one can be mistaken in what one believes, that one can as easily believe that one knows something when one does not know it as one can believe anything else to be so when it is not so.

If belief is not sufficient for knowledge, is it *necessary?* Many philosophers who would agree that knowledge does not in any way imply certainty, would, nevertheless, insist that knowledge does imply belief. And this in one or both of two ways. To know something, they hold, implies that one *believes it* and/or that one *believes that one knows it.* Some[11] would, indeed, add that one must not only believe, but also know, that one knows what one knows.

The latter thesis, namely, that one must believe (and, perhaps, even know) that one knows what in fact one does know makes sense whatever one knows, whether it is knowing that the earth goes round the sun, where the treasure is buried, how to play Canasta, the date of the Battle of the Boyne or one's next door neighbour. Hence, it is an arguable question—and one that I shall discuss—whether the thesis is always, sometimes or never true.

The former thesis, namely that one must believe that which one knows, on the other hand, clearly only makes sense for some of the things one can know and clearly, though making sense, need not be true for other things one can know. First, someone who knows that the earth goes round the sun can also believe this, whereas it makes no sense to say that someone who knows where the treasure is buried believes where it is buried or that someone who knows how to play Canasta believes how to play it or that someone who knows the date of the Battle of the Boyne believes the date. Nevertheless, since knowing where something is implies knowing that it is in the place in which in fact it is, knowing how to play Canasta implies knowing that so and so is the way to play it and knowing the date of something implies knowing that it occurred at the time at which it did in fact occur, and since these things which are implied are all things one can believe, one could stretch the thesis that one must believe what one knows to cover knowledge of these items. Secondly, though it makes sense to say that someone believes the people he knows and believes the stories he knows, it clearly is not either necessary or, perhaps, even common that it should be true that he believes them. Thirdly, it does not make sense to ask whether someone who knows a locality, such as London or the Camargue, or who has known a condition, such as suffering, great joy or galloping inflation, believes or did believe what he knows or knew.

Since, therefore, the thesis that one necessarily believes that one knows what in fact one does know is wider than the thesis that one necessarily believes what one knows and since the reasons for and against the former thesis are basically the same as those for and against that part of the latter which straightforwardly makes sense, namely, that, if one knows that p, one believes that p, I will begin by examining the former thesis.

(i) BELIEVING THAT ONE KNOWS

One reason for the thesis that to know something implies to believe that one knows it is the confusion between knowing and claiming to know which I discussed in Chapter 1. It is the confusion[12] of the real impossibility of properly (justifiably, sensibly, consistently, honestly, sincerely, etc.,) *saying* "I know" and at the same time *saying* "I do not think that I know" with the alleged impossibility of *knowing* something and at the same time *not believing* that one knows it. Philosophers who would, in this day and age, never dream of confusing the paradoxicality of "Tomorrow is Tuesday, but I don't think it is" with the logical possibility of tomorrow's being Tuesday although someone, even the speaker, does not think it is, are still prone to assimilate the impropriety of saying "I know but I don't think (know) I know" to the alleged impossibility of knowing without thinking (knowing) one knows and/or to shift deliberately from the latter problem to the former.

Sometimes this confusion takes the form of assimilating the conditions of knowing something to the conditions of a justified claim to know something and, therefore, arguing from the plausibility that one who justifiably claims to know something must be convinced of his claim to know it (and of what he claimed to know) to the conclusion that someone who knows something must be convinced that he knows it (and of what he knows). Similarly, it is sometimes supposed[13] that if someone knows something he must not only be able to give the correct answer to a question, but be able to show that his answer is correct. And if he does this, it is difficult to see how he could avoid believing his answer. This supposition, however, is the point at issue and I shall give examples to show how it is possible for someone to know things, which are, therefore, correct, without knowing that they are correct.

But, as we saw in Chapter 1, the reasons why someone who says that he knows something implies or suggests by saying this that he thinks or is convinced that he does know it do not show that what he says—or the fact, whether stated or unstated—carries any such implication. To suppose otherwise would be like supposing quite implausibly that because to say that one does *not* know something implies that one thinks one does *not* know it, therefore *not* knowing something implies thinking that one does *not* know it. Saying that one knows that there is life on Mars implies or suggests that one thinks that one knows there is for exactly the same reason that saying that there is life on Mars implies or suggests that one thinks there is; whereas clearly there is no implication or suggestion in what is said, or in the fact, i.e., that there is life on Mars, that anyone thinks that there is. Any suggestion or implication carried by one's saying something—or by one's doing something—is not necessarily carried by what is said. This is why we can restrict the suggestion or implication of someone's saying something to his saying it sincerely, for the purpose of informing, etc., as opposed to his saying it to deceive, in a play, etc.; whereas it makes no sense to ask whether the fact itself was sincere, in a play, etc. Saying that something is so is the normal way of expressing one's belief that it is so. Hence, if one does not think either that p or that one knows that p one won't, except for some ulterior motive, say either that p or that one knows that p. Saying sincerely that one knows something is good evidence that one thinks, or is convinced, that one knows it, but not that one does know it; and feeling unable to say sincerely that one knows is good evidence that one does not think that one knows, but not that one does not know.

A second reason for the thesis under consideration is a traditional assumption that knowing something is being in a certain state of mind, which, therefore, one must know whether one is in or not. To this the objections are, first, that even if knowing something were being in a state of mind, it does not follow that one must think, much less know, that one is in that state anymore than one must necessarily think or know that one is jealous or envious when one is; and, secondly, and more importantly, that knowledge of something is not a state of mind. For instance, feeling knowledgeable is not related to being knowledgeable as feeling jealous or afraid is to being jealous or afraid. Feeling knowledgeable is not a feeling of knowledge, but a feeling that one has knowledge. There are not characteristic bodily expressions of knowledge as there are of mental states. There is a legitimate query why someone is in a certain state, but not why he knows and a different legitimate query how he knows but not how he is in the state he is in. The methods of finding out whether someone knows something are roughly the same whether the examinee is one's self or another, but the methods of finding out whether one's self is in a certain state differ both from those of finding out whether one's self or another knows something and from those of finding out whether another is in a certain state. Whatever the plausibility of supposing that one can find out by introspection whether one is in a particular state of mind, it is simply a mistake to suppose that introspection must be able to show one whether one knew, e.g., the names of all the Derby winners or whether one only thought one did.

Just as this common philosophical argument against the possibility of knowledge without conviction is based on a mis-classification of knowledge as a state of mind, so Schopenhauer's argument[14] against it, namely that any attempt to try to know without knowing that one knows or *vice-versa* necessarily fails, mis-classifies knowing as something one can try to do.

Related to this assumption that knowledge is a state of mind is a failure to appreciate how utterly different are the concepts of conviction (or belief) and knowledge. To be convinced, unlike to know, is to be in a certain state of mind. Hence, unlike knowledge, it is something we can feel, something which has characteristic bodily expressions and behaviour. Conviction is a disposition to behave, but knowledge is more akin to an ability. A conviction that p, but not knowledge that p, necessarily involves a readiness to assert that p. One can ask why, but not how, one is convinced and how, but not why, one knows. Wondering whether or not one knows is vastly more common than wondering whether or not one is convinced. An increase or decrease in conviction is an increase or decrease in its intensity; an increase or decrease in knowledge is in its extent. Hence, one's conviction about a specific point can alter; but only one's knowledge about an area or details. Acquiring, losing or regaining one's conviction about something is quite different from acquiring, losing or regaining one's knowledge of it. To have moments or even days of doubt about something is not necessarily to have moments or even days of forgetfulness about it. As we shall see, the sorts of things, like apparent counter-examples, psychological pressures, changes of character, which sow seeds of doubt in one's mind are quite different from the sorts of things, like distractions, disuse, panic, lack of practice, intrinsic difficulty of the material, which make one forget things. The fact that convincing a man that he does not know something will often serve the same purpose as erasing knowledge of it from his mind does not show that the two are the same.

Not only is conviction of, or belief in, knowledge quite compatible with lack of knowledge, there is no concomitant variation between conviction and knowledge. Because the causes of doubt

are in general different from the causes of ignorance or forgetfulness, conviction can increase or decrease without any effect on
one's knowledge. Just as I don't remember what I have temporarily forgotten, much less come to know what I was previously
ignorant of, merely because of an increase in my conviction that I
do not know, so I don't forget all I know because of an increased
doubt whether I do know it. I don't know something better because
I am more confident of knowing it. Doubts and convictions are
typically things that often come and go rapidly because they depend much on changing circumstances, both internal and external,
whereas knowledge is fairly steadfast and usually only eroded by
time. Knowledge consists in the possession of abilities of various
kinds. Like anything else one possesses, these are things whose
possession one may, for various reasons, forget, fail to realise, not
recognise, be unaware, unsure or unconvinced of, or be doubtful,
dubious or hesitant of.

So different are the concepts of knowledge and conviction of, or
belief in, knowledge that neither implies the other. No one, of
course, supposes that being convinced, or believing, that one
knows something either implies that one knows it or even that this
is sufficient evidence that one knows it. Unjustified confidence is
all too common. Symbolically, BK $\not\vdash$ K. This truth is just as clear in
its contrapositive form. Not all who lack knowledge of a particular
matter are necessarily either convinced of their ignorance or free
from all belief that they may have the answer. Symbolically, $\bar{K} \not\vdash \sim$
(BK), whether $\sim$ (BK) is taken as $B\bar{K}$ or as $\bar{B}K$.

Equally, if less obviously, knowing something does not imply
being convinced, or thinking, that one knows it; nor, contrapositively, does not thinking that one knows it imply that one does
not know it. It makes perfectly good sense to say that someone
knows something where he is not convinced, or perhaps does not
even think, that he knows; whether "not thinking that one knows
something" is interpreted as "not-thinking that one knows" or as
"thinking that one does not know." Symbolically, K $\not\vdash$ BK and,
hence, $\sim$ (BK) $\not\vdash \bar{K}$, whether $\sim$ (BK) is taken as $B\bar{K}$ or as $\bar{B}K$.

Thus, I may never feel quite sure—and for this reason say each
time I'm asked that I never know—whether the tropic of Cancer is
north or south of the tropic of Capricorn or whether Napoleon's

second exile was on Elba or St. Helena. But all the evidence may show that I undoubtedly do know and on the very infrequent occasions on which I am asked get the answer right. Faced with an unfamiliar looking example, the school boy, the trainee locksmith or the guest in the intellectual party game may wonder whether, or even deny that, he knows how to solve this one, and find that, for all his doubt or denial, he does. Neither any lack of conviction about my ability nor any conviction of my inability to recite the names of the Kings of England, the dates of Marlborough's victories or all the stanzas of the Ancient Mariner shows that I lack this ability. I may think that I don't know or not think that I do know the new Minister of Defence until you remind me that we were at school together. My hesitation about the voice on the distorted record does not show that it isn't the well loved and well known voice of my daughter. My failure to recognise my friend may convince me that he is someone I don't know or make me uncertain whether he is someone I do know. My knowledge that Terence's line reads "Humani nil a me alienum puto" is usually accompanied by a lot of doubt because of the many variant misquotations and misattributions of it I have seen since I last looked it up many years ago. If knowing something did imply thinking that one knows it, that is, if $K > BK$, then one might expect—though it does not, of course, follow—that not knowing something might imply thinking that one does not know it, that is, $\bar{K} > B\bar{K}$. But clearly there are countless things I don't know about which I have never wondered whether I know them or not and, therefore, which I probably don't think I don't know. Even among those things I don't know of which I have wondered whether I know them or not, there are many which I wrongly thought I did know and which, therefore, are not likely to be things which I thought I did not know.

Furthermore, the alleged impossibility or infrequency of knowing something without thinking that one knows it would rule out any occasion for the use of such phrases as "wondering, doubting, making sure, being not certain" that I know something, whether what is in question is knowing where, when or what something is, or how, where or when to do something.

The basic cause, however, for the persistence of the view that knowledge either cannot be or never is without conviction or belief in it is the frequency of their co-existence. What I wish to argue, however, is that the explanation of this lies not in any conceptual or necessary connection between knowledge and conviction or belief, but in the varied and changing circumstances in which we acquire, retain, lose or try to produce our knowledge. Just as we can explain why someone should sometimes feel convinced that he knows what he could not know, so we can explain both why he should often feel convinced that he knows what he does know and also why he should sometimes have this knowledge without this conviction.

The methods by which we acquire our knowledge of things, whether by perception of them, by working out answers, by rote learning and practice, by acceptance of the authority of persons or books, often give us at the same time a belief or conviction both in what we have acquired and in our acquisition of it. In coming to know something we often also come to know, believe and be convinced, that we have come to know it, just as when seeing something we usually realise and are sure that we have seen it. What gives a man knowledge often also gives him conviction both that he knows and of what he knows. The more recent, the more frequently used, the more prominent or in some other way the more important the knowledge, the more likely is it that one retains also this belief or conviction of the knowledge acquired. It is not surprising that one who knows that London is the biggest city in England, where Glasgow is, who won the Battle of Waterloo, how to do long division or the names of his own children is also quite convinced, and indeed knows, that he knows all this. It is a diet of such standard examples that often leads philosophers to suppose that knowing implies being convinced, believing, or even knowing, that one knows.

Equally, however, there are all sorts of causal reasons why one should sometimes not be convinced, or even believe, that one knows something which one undoubtedly does know. What undermines one's confidence may, but need not, obliterate one's knowledge.

With the passage of time and the lack of use of that knowledge, one may have forgotten that or how one acquired it without forgetting that which was acquired. I may still know how the subjunctive is used in Greek—after all, I once took a degree in Classics—but time and disuse have weakened any conviction I ever had that I do know this. If you ask me what I know about the use of the subjunctive in Greek, I will certainly hesitate before committing myself. If, when I tell you all I can immediately recollect, you ask whether this is all I know about it, I am not sure whether it is. Moreover, I am more sure of some of what I know about the subjunctive than of other parts of what I know about it. There are a host of skills, abilities and aptitudes I once possessed. I used to know how to swim, ride a bicycle, tie a bowline, extract square roots, etc. I have not had occasion to do any of these things for many years. I don't know and am not at all sure whether I still know how to do them. People tell me that these are things one never forgets; but I am not convinced. Shall I try it? On the other hand, there is plenty of evidence that if someone knows how to do one thing he knows how to do another thing very like the former. Yet, here are you and I, faced with the question whether we know how to solve this equation, open this safe, handle this situation. As a matter of fact, we both do know, as subsequent events prove, but you are sure you do, while I am not at all convinced that I do. Nor can one properly escape this conclusion by arguing that one does not know how to do something now until one actually does it. This would be like arguing, incorrectly, that one cannot do something until one does it. It may not be until I start helping my son with his homework that I realise or become convinced that I really know much less or much more of what I learnt at school than I thought I did. A further instance of the way in which the passage of time may make me unsure or unaware that I know something which indeed I do know is exemplified in the way that hypnotism may enable me to come to see what I learnt as a child but could not recall. Hypnotism does not reteach me or enable me to relearn what I once knew but have now forgotten, it makes me aware of what I have known all along. Indeed, such knowledge may consciously have been the present cause of the difficulties which persuaded me to see a psychiatrist.

Or the lack of conviction may be due to a, perhaps temporary, inability to recognise what I know as something I know. Looking at the familiar object, person or problem in an unfamiliar light or being given an inadequate description of it, I may well not know what it is and, therefore, be convinced, as Plato suggested at one place in the *Theaetetus*, that it is not something I know. Those philosophers[15] who consider knowledge analogous to sight nevertheless overlook the fact that, though in this analogy normally we are sure that we see what we see, we can see something in so unfamiliar a guise that we do not realise or believe that we have seen it. Also, just as you can see what is in fact my brother Harry and not know that you see my brother Harry, so you can know the occupation of one of my brothers—in fact it's my brother Harry—and not know that you know the occupation of my brother Harry.

Equally, though knowing that X is Y does not imply knowing that Z is Y even when X is Z—e.g., knowing that the robber is the murderer does not imply knowing that your neighbour is the murderer even though the robber is your neighbour—since one may not know that X is Z (that the robber is your neighbour), yet knowing how to V does imply knowing how to F, if to V is to F, even though one does not know that to V is to F—e.g., one who knows how to waylay his neighbour knows how to waylay the murderer, if his neighbour is the murderer, even though he does not know that to waylay his neighbour is to waylay the murderer and, therefore, does not know that he knows how to waylay the murderer.

As well as failure to recognise some of one's knowledge when one sees it, there may be failure to recollect, recall, summon up or list some of this knowledge. So that even if it were true—which I've suggested it is not—that whenever one did recall it one would recognise it as something one knew and, therefore, be convinced that one knew it, no such conviction about it is felt at the moment. Neither momentary failure to remember nor momentary inability to think of something implies lack of knowledge of it. We all amass an enormous amount of knowledge during our lives, some of it of so minor a character and so often unrecalled that, as Plato tries to bring out with his analogy of the aviary in the *Theaetetus*, we cannot be sure whether we have it or not. I am not sure that I know his home telephone number, her maiden name, the time of the meeting; nor even that I know anyone of that name or know of anyone with a spare copy of that book. Young children are often told, as Socrates assured the slave boy in the *Meno,* that they know the answers to questions despite their own lack of conviction. Just as some people don't know as much as they think they know, so others know more than they think they do. It's because experience has taught him that witnesses, especially in the shock of the moment, usually know more than they think they do, that the policeman's parting request is to be told immediately if they should think of anything else.

Here is one reason[16] for the difference between the quite common lack of conviction whether I know what or where something is, how or when to do something, the name, size or weight of something and the much rarer feeling of uncertainty about my knowledge that p. For when you ask me whether I know something in the other examples you don't remind me of the answer; whereas when you ask me whether I know that p, you at the same time refresh my mind. Similarly, when I ask myself. But even here I am not always sure. Did I know that Jane's divorce had come through, or that John had got a reply from the Gas Board? I have a feeling that I did, but I'm not sure. My wife often upbraids me for arranging a meeting for an evening when, she indignantly assures me, I knew that she had invited the Jones's round. Naturally, if and when I go so far as to commit myself to a firm answer, e.g., to your question where, how or when did so-and-so happen, it is even less likely that I have not the slightest belief that it is right. It is partly because philosophers commonly restrict themselves to such cases that they fail to find knowledge without belief. The fact that the man who volunteers the correct date of the Battle of Waterloo, because he actually does know the date, may have some feeling, whatever he says to the contrary, that that is the date does not show that someone cannot know the date without at the time either thinking that a particular date is right or thinking that he knows which date is right, for he may at that time not volunteer any date. Hence, though "I don't think I know that p" is much rarer than "I don't think I know where or what it is, how or when to do it," both can be true even when I do know. *A fortiori,* I can know that p, as well as know where or what something is, without being convinced that I do, when I'm not reminded by you nor do I remind myself what the thing is. If I know what her maiden name is and her name is Burgoyne, then I know that her maiden name is Burgoyne.

Though often, of course, I am only contrasting a temporary lack of certainty with a long-term knowledge, it is not always like this. Often also my loss of conviction has itself a long history, so that I've long known something which either I've long doubted I knew or about which I have long had no view either way. It's many years since I have had any feeling of conviction—or perhaps feelings of any kind—about my knowledge of the Greek subjunctive. Until I pleasantly surprised myself with my answers to my son's questions about co-ordinate geometry, I had been for years firmly convinced that I'd lost all my knowledge of this topic. Not every loss of conviction is momentary.

Even when the things I know well have not become dimmed with age or hidden by disguise, there are several reasons why I should lack conviction or even be filled with doubt whether I know them. Perhaps strange circumstances breed the doubts. I could have sworn that I know exactly where something is at the moment— and, indeed, I do know—but the reports about its appearance in other places make me doubt my knowledge. Someone debauched by too much reading of sceptical philosophy may well come to think that neither he nor anyone else knows or even can know what—since the sceptics' arguments are fallacious—we all certainly do know.[17] Or perhaps I'm diffident or even neurotically sceptical by nature. Unlike my fellows, I'm not at all convinced that I know all of what I do know. Am I sure I do know the time of the train? Perhaps I'd better look it up again. Or maybe I'm under an emotional strain. Most students go through a period before their examinations when they begin to doubt the extent of their knowledge.

Or psychological attempts may have been made to shake my confidence. The nervous witness, who has been subjected to an hour's crossexamination by a clever or hectoring counsel, may be so filled with doubts as to withdraw his early confident claim that he did know the accused or know what he was carrying near the scene of the crime. But, despite the counsel's insinuations to the jury, the witness's loss of confidence in his testimony no more shows that he no longer knows or never did know what he earlier confidently claimed to know than it does that he did not see what he earlier confidently claimed to see. Shaking a man's confidence does not make him forget what he knows or show that he never knew it at all.

Nor, indeed, is all acquisition of knowledge necessarily also a beginning of belief or confidence in that knowledge. I can be correctly informed of something without being persuaded of it. I can fail to recognise a discovery at the time I make it. Just as I sometimes think I have proved what I have not, so I can refuse to believe, or be unwilling or unable to believe, that I have proved what I have proved. Not every student believes what he is taught even when what he has been taught is the truth. And if there are strange or inexplicable ways of acquiring knowledge, by telepathy, clairvoyance, intuition, etc., someone may be possessed of one of these without believing that he is and, therefore, without believing that he has acquired any knowledge when one of these suggests an answer to him. Whether what we acquire in all these circumstances is knowledge depends on the correctness of what is acquired and the means by which it was acquired, but not on our conviction or lack of it either at the moment of acquisition or subsequently.

It might be objected[18] that if one who is not sure that he knows something or even thinks that he does not know it can in fact know it, so one who is not sure that he thinks so and so or even thinks that he does not think it can nevertheless think it. Hence, it is added, the fact that someone says and is sure that he does not think he knows so and so does not show that he does not in fact think he knows it. We cannot, therefore, rely merely on his being sure that he does not think he knows something, much less on his not being sure that he does think he knows it, to prove that he does not think he knows it. Admittedly, there is a difference between saying, however sincerely—or even being sure—that one does not think, or believe, so and so and really thinking, or believing, this. Actions often, though not always, speak louder than words, so that what one does may, though it need not, be a clearer indication of what one thinks than what one says even to oneself. Thus, my saying, however sincerely, that I don't think women are inferior to men may be belied by my behaviour towards them. Nor does the failure to give any specific thought to the question, of whether women are inferior to men, show that one does not have a particular belief on the subject.[19] In order, however, to use this legitimate distinction to show that one who says or is sure that he does not think he knows may nevertheless really think he knows, one must produce other evidence that he does really think he knows; for against this we have his present feeling of certainty that he does not think he knows, his unwillingness to say that he knows and his failure to do any of the things that a man who thinks he knows could be expected to do. For we must not use as evidence that he thinks he knows any of those things—such as his successful performance—that would be merely evidence that he knows, since this would beg the question whether knowing something implies thinking one knows it.

I have argued that the reason why one who knows something does not necessarily or invariably believe that he knows what he knows is the variety of and change in the circumstances in which he acquired, retained or is called on to produce this knowledge. It is not, as several philosophers[20] have alleged, some ambiguity of language giving rise to two senses of "know," one of which allegedly does and the other does not imply belief; nor is it because knowledge without belief is, as has also been alleged,[21] only a borderline case of knowledge.

It is not necessary to add an elaborate proof that just as one can know something without believing that one does know it, so one can know something without knowing that one does know it. Against those who hold that to know something implies to believe that one knows it, any instance of knowing something without believing that one knows it would, *a fortiori,* be an instance of knowing something without knowing that one knows it. Clearly, however, since I have disputed the assumption that to know something implies to believe that one knows it, I cannot use this assumption to disprove that to know something implies to know that one knows it. That this latter is false can, nevertheless, easily be shown—as, indeed, I have hinted at several places in the above argument—in an analogous way to that in which it has been shown that it is false that to know something implies to believe that one

knows it. Anyone who is induced, in any of the above circumstances, to hold the wrong answer to the question "Do you know
so and so?" does not know that he knows so and so.

(II) BELIEVING WHAT ONE KNOWS

Let us now turn to the more commonly[22] held and more traditional
thesis that to know something implies believing that which is
known. We have already seen that in order to be at all plausible,
this thesis must be restricted in several ways. First, "knowing
where, when, what, how something V's", only involves belief in so
far as it also involves knowing that so and so is the place, time,
thing or way it V's, and "knowing where, when, what, how to do
something" only involves belief in so far as it involves knowing
that so and so is the place, time or way to do something or the thing
to do. Secondly, the thesis, though making sense, is clearly false, if
it asserts that knowing a person or a story implies believing him or
it. Thirdly, it cannot be applied to the object known in knowing a
locality or condition, such as London or great suffering.

On the other hand, there are two *prima facie* objections to the
thesis which can be rejected. The first is that made by Plato long
ago and by Zeno Vendler recently, that knowing something cannot
imply believing it, on the ground that what is known cannot be
believed and what is believed cannot be known. For Plato, it will
be remembered, what is known is the world of Forms and what is
believed the world of appearances; for Vendler what is known is
reality and what is believed are propositions. We have earlier
refuted this objection.

We can even more easily dismiss a second *prima facie* objection,
namely, that common remarks like "I don't believe it, I know it" or
"It's not a question of believing, I actually know" show that
knowledge not only does not imply belief, but is even incompatible
with it. For what the remarks contrast is not belief and knowledge
but "mere" belief and knowledge, just as "It's not big, it's huge"
or "It's not difficult, it's impossible" mean that the first description
is an understatement, only a part of what the second description
mentions more fully or more accurately. Nor should we conclude[23]
that because knowledge and belief are quite different kinds of

concepts, therefore they mutually exclude each other and, hence, knowledge does not merely not imply belief, it implies the absence of belief. Truth (or reality) and knowledge are quite different kinds of concepts, yet knowledge does not exclude truth (or reality).

As I stressed earlier, the thesis that knowing something implies believing it is not the same as the thesis that knowing that p implies believing that p, since the latter thesis, but not the former, is compatible with the view that what is known when it is known that p is not the same as what is believed when it is believed that p. While the former thesis holds that knowing something implies believing *it,* the latter holds only that knowing something implies believing *something,* whether the same thing or another. Nevertheless, philosophers who discuss the latter clearly mean it to be taken as an instance of the former. No one, as far as I know, has bothered about the vague view that knowing something implies believing something or other. Further, many of the arguments against the former count also against the latter. Finally, it is the former, not the latter, that is under examination. To it there are at least two sets of objections.

First, the thesis borrows much of its plausibility from the fact that someone who sincerely claimed or asserted that he knew something would not do so unless he believed it; for why should he have put it forward as something he knew unless it was also something he believed. Hence, it is significant that those philosophers[24] who make belief a necessary condition of knowledge are those who attempt an analysis not of knowledge, but of claims to knowledge. But, there can be and are occasions when someone knows something on which, nevertheless, he does not claim or assert that he knows it and on which, therefore, this argument cannot be used to show that he believes it.

Secondly, many of the arguments used to show that knowing something does not imply believing that you know it also show that it does not imply believing it itself; and *vice versa.* Thus, many of the circumstances that lead one to cease to believe or even to doubt that one knows something commonly lead one also to cease to believe or even to doubt the thing itself. The circumstances of its acquisition, the passage of time, the intricate detail or the unfamiliar guise of the subject matter, the ingenious arguments used against its truth, one's own natural diffidence or the brow-beating of opposing counsel may make one both doubt one's knowledge of something and even doubt its own status. Nor need what leads me to cease to believe or even to doubt something lead me so far as to believe the opposite. Not all cases of not believing that p can be turned into cases of believing that not-p.[25]

Admittedly, the possibility of knowing something without believing that one knows it, that is K.B̄K, does not imply the possibility of knowing it without believing it, that is, K.B̄, for someone may not think that he knows something—e.g., because he cannot prove it to himself—of which nevertheless he is quite sure and which, unknown to him, he does in fact know. Nevertheless, the truth of the former does at least strengthen the plausibility of the latter.

I conclude, therefore, that there is no good reason for accepting the thesis that knowledge implies belief either in the form that one must believe that one knows that which one does in fact know or in the form that one must believe that which one knows.

Since, as we have seen, being right is a necessary but not a sufficient condition for knowledge, while belief is neither necessary nor sufficient, it follows that the combination of correctness and belief cannot be necessary. Can such a combination be sufficient? In some contexts, as we saw, either it does not *prima facie* make sense or can clearly be false to talk of correctly believing what one knows, as when one knows where, when or how something V's or where, when or how to V something, when one knows pain or poverty or when one knows a person or place. Here, therefore, the suggestion clearly will not work. But, quite apart from these contexts, it is easy to show, as Plato realised long ago in the *Meno* (97 c) and the *Theaetetus,* that someone can correctly believe something, e.g., that 1690 was the date of the Battle of the Boyne or that the oil tank is half full, though he does not know this, since his correct belief was arrived at in a way, such as by guessing, by luck, by fallacious reasoning or by several mutually cancelling miscalculations or misobservations, which does not allow it to count as knowledge. As Plato observed, the jury does not know what happened at the scene of the crime, if their belief about the events, however correct, is due only to specious arguments and false evidence put forward by the defence. Furthermore, it makes sense[26] to say that one can correctly and firmly, hesitatingly or reluctantly believe, but not that one can in any of these ways know, that p.

D. JUSTIFICATION

Because the criteria of correctness and belief were seen to be jointly insufficient, even for those who consider them necessary, for knowledge, a third criterion has traditionally been offered. Plato in the *Theaetetus* called this *logos*, though he could offer no version of it which even he found satisfactory. More recently, it has been usual to argue that, in addition to being correct, a man's belief in something must be *justified* before he can be said to know it. Hence, it is sometimes[27] held that in order to know something, one must have a right to be sure of what one correctly believes or, more commonly,[28] that knowledge is logically equivalent to justified true belief. Some[29] allege a "weak" and a "strong" sense of "know" where the former is equivalent merely to "true belief."

Clearly, however, if my previous arguments are correct that neither belief nor certainty is necessary for knowledge, then neither true belief with the right to be sure nor justified true belief can be necessary for knowledge. It is significant that much of the discussion of and adherence to the notion of justification occurs not in relation to the nature of knowledge, but in relation to claims or assertions of knowledge.[30] It is reasonable to ask for some justification for someone's claim to know something or for his belief in it, as it is reasonable to ask with what right he is so sure about it. But, as I argued earlier, someone may know something without claiming to know it and even without believing either it or that he knows it.

Not only is a justified true belief not necessary for knowledge, it is also not sufficient.[31] This is shown partly by our everyday use of the two notions.[32] We often contrast the time at which we have excellent reasons for believing that p and the later time at which we know or can prove that p and we often contrast those who at a given time have such reasons for believing that p and those others who at the same time know that p. I may have been fully justified in suspecting something which I now finally know because I've seen it; and you may have the best of reasons for believing something about me which only I can know. Knowledge is often distinguished from justified true belief by a piece of clinching evidence.

The insufficiency of justified true belief for knowledge can also be shown in a rather more esoteric way,[33] which basically relies[34] on the fact that one can be as justified in believing what is not so (or false) as one can in believing what is so (or true) and, therefore, one can be justified in believing what is right for reasons which one could not have known were wrong. Thus, to use a variation on a type of example popularised by Gettier, but earlier mentioned by Plato[35] and Russell:[36] if A is justified in believing that p, e.g., that his host at a party was talking to Obolensky, and is justified in believing (or perhaps knows) that p implies q, e.g., that if he was talking to Obolensky, he was talking to a Russian, then he is justified in believing that q, e.g., that he was talking to a Russian. But if p is false and it is true that p implies q, then q does not follow from them and could be either true or false. If q, however, happens to be true, then A is both justified and correct in believing that q, though the way he arrived at this belief, that is, by use of a false premise, would lead us to deny that he knew, had discovered, proved or found out the answer.

Attempts may be made to meet this objection by so tightening up the idea of justification that either one cannot be justified in believing anything unless it is actually implied by the evidence for one's belief[37] or one cannot be justified in believing anything simply because it is implied by something else one is justified in believing.[38]

The result of the first attempt is that the objection cannot go through because, according to this attempt, one cannot be justified in believing what is not so (or false). Such a restricted criterion of justification is, however, false to the actual use of the idea of justification. The result of the second attempt is that the notion of being justified in believing something is not necessarily, as perhaps the original objection assumed, transitive. This might happen in two ways with significantly different analogues in the notion of probability. Thus, in the first case, if one has adequate, but not a lot of, justification for believing that p, e.g., that the man in room 6 is dead, and equally adequate, though different, justification for believing that q, e.g., that the man in room 6 is my brother, it does not follow that one has adequate justification for believing what is implied by p and q, that is, that my brother is dead in the room, just as, if the probability that p is greater than ½, say ⅔ and the probability that q is greater than ½, say ⅔, then the probability that p and q, which is 4⁄9, is not necessarily greater than ½.

In the second case, if one is justified in believing that p, e.g., that one's host is talking to the Russian Obolensky, is one justified in believing that p or q, which follows from p—e.g., that either he is talking to Obolensky or to some other Russian, that is, that he is talking to a Russian? Certainly, if the probability that p is ½, then the probability that p or q is equal to or greater than ½. Since p or q can be true, even if p is false, provided q is true, one's belief that one's friend is talking either to the Russian Obolensky or to some other Russian, that is, that he is talking to a Russian, might seem to be a justified true belief, though the element of it which is true is not the element which one is justified in believing. At most one believes what is right for the wrong reason. This is analogous to the way in which, if I mark a target and you hit the target, then you hit what I mark, that is the target, though you need not hit the part of the target which I mark.

I conclude, therefore, that justified true belief is neither a necessary nor a sufficient condition of knowledge. Furthermore, though attempts to add to the criteria may eventually produce a set which are jointly sufficient—even if no such attempt has yet won general acceptance[39]—such attempts must, if the arguments of the earlier chapters are correct, fail to produce a set of necessary criteria and, therefore, a correct analysis of knowledge.

E. ROUTE

What, I think, the criterion of justification has confused is the method or means by which someone acquired his knowledge, that is, actually came into possession of his information, brought off his achievement, or became familiar with the object of his acquaintance, and the method or means by which he arrived, or could legitimately have arrived, at a belief in what he knows. Whether someone knows something or claims to know it, it is natural to wonder or ask *how* he knows it and to suppose that if there is no way by which he came to know it, then he does not in fact know it at all. If he claims or believes that he knows it, then we seek a justification of this claim or belief by demanding an account of the route by which he in fact did, or anyone legitimately could, come to have it. But whether his attempt to justify his claim is mistaken or whether he makes no attempt because he makes no claim, the important point is not either his route to a belief or his belief in a route to knowledge—for this could only justify him in claiming what he does—but what in fact was his route, or is a possible route, to knowledge. What the numerous attempts to make a justified true belief not only a necessary but also a sufficient condition of knowledge really seek is the addition of some restriction on the acceptable means, methods, reasoning, etc., by which one reaches one's belief. In fact, however, if one gets one's hold on reality—or hits upon the truth—by certain means, it will be allowed that one knows, whether or not one can give the correct or any account of these things. If one has not acquired it by these means, one's reasons for supposing it to be reality will be irrelevant.

It is because we think that there is no way in which someone could have known so and so—e.g., he was not there, he was deaf, the evidence was destroyed, it was before his time, he used a false premise, he miscalculated, etc.,—or that there is no way in which anyone could have known—e.g., it was the secret thoughts of another, it was in the future, it is contrary to the laws of physics or of chance—that we conclude either that he did not know—it was a lucky guess, a happy thought—or that he acquired the knowledge in some mysterious way, e.g., telepathy, clairvoyance, precognition, extra-sensory perception, intuition, supernatural vision, divine communion, etc.

Sceptical philosophers take various rather restrictive views as to what are legitimate routes, ways, methods or means to the acquisition of knowledge. Thus, as we saw, they often restrict them to those deductive routes, where the conclusions necessarily follow, to those we can personally experience or to those composed of what is contemporaneous with the traveller. But the answer really depends not on philosophical theories,[40] but on the nature of the knowledge acquired. Thus, though the expert's knowledge of mathematics is ultimately acquired by reasoning, a particular individual's knowledge may be due to having read the answer in an authoritative text book or having had it from someone who knows. Scientific knowledge is not restricted to deductive methods of acquisition. Like our knowledge of everyday facts, it is reached by perception, by reading, by being told, by experimentation, etc. It is a debatable question whether there are other, so far inexplicable, routes, such as telepathy, clairvoyance, or intuition.

Incidentally, though all philosophers who number either the right to be sure or being justified in believing among their criteria for knowledge insist on actual belief or certainty as another criterion, it is both possible and meaningful to demand a right to be sure without demanding that one actually be sure and possible, though doubtfully meaningful, to demand that one be justified in believing what one does not actually believe. Hence, it is possible to ask whether the right to be sure or being justified in believing is by itself a necessary condition of knowledge and/or whether in combination with either reality (or truth) or belief it is a necessary or a sufficient condition. Taken thus, a right to be sure or a justification in believing might be advanced merely as alternative versions of what I have called a legitimate way, means or method or an accredited route.[41] This would, however, be very dubious, since there need be no suggestion that the person who knows something is aware of the route by which he came to know it; yet the mere existence of the route would not be sufficient to give someone the right to be sure of or be justified in believing his conclusion. He would, at least, have to be aware of the route, even though such awareness failed somehow to make him actually sure. To be justified in believing so and so, it would not be sufficient for the proper evidence for the conclusion to exist; he would need to possess it, though failing somehow to realise it.

Nor should the necessity of some way, means, method or route by which one came to know, discover, learn or get hold of something be interpreted as the *cause* either of his knowing, learning, discovering, etc., or of his believing what he knows, has learnt or discovered. Though something can *enable* one to know or discover as it can enable one to see or in some other way perceive, such things cannot *cause* one to know any more than they can cause one to see. The stepping stones which enable me to cross the stream do not cause me to cross it, nor do the earphones which enable me to hear the music cause me to hear it. To cause something to V is to make it V; to enable it to V is to make it possible for it to V. On the other hand, whereas something can cause one to believe so and so—though one's reason for believing need not be a cause[42]—just as it can cause it to look to someone as if so and so is such and such, believing that p is, as we saw, neither necessary nor sufficient for knowing that p anymore than it's looking to someone that something is so and so is either necessary or sufficient for one's seeing so and so. Furthermore, what enables one to know, learn or discover that p, just as what enables one to see X, is not the fact that p or X itself,[43] but something which puts one in contact with the fact that p or with X, e.g., having been authoritatively told, having calculated, experimented, reasoned, etc., that p or having experienced such and such. Even more clearly, it is not, e.g., how, where or when *to* V that enables us to know these; nor does it make sense to say that they cause us to believe these, for we cannot, as we saw, believe them. The causal theory of knowledge is open to the same kinds of objections[44] as the causal theory of perception on which it is admittedly[45] founded. Just as the causal theory of perception has to presuppose that in perceiving one has sense-data which are caused, so the causal theory of knowledge has to presuppose that in knowing one has beliefs which are caused.[46] In fact, the so-called causal theory of knowledge is really a causal theory of belief just as its parent, the causal theory of perception, is really a causal theory of perceptual experience. But what needs to be explained is *how* we got to know so and so, not *why* we believe it. I can, as we saw, learn something, e.g., some geography at school or some unsavoury fact about a colleague, without anything's causing me to believe it at the time I came to know it.

I conclude, therefore, that the jointly necessary and sufficient criteria for knowledge are, first, that it is a grasp on reality, whether of how things are or how to do things and, secondly, that this grasp on reality was obtained by an accredited route, e.g., by experience, deduction, perception, calculation, authority, etc., or at least *not* by guess work, chance, luck, accident, etc.[47] Lately, a good deal of energy has been expended by philosophers[48] in attempts to devise a watertight formula, impervious to a series of ingenious and far-fetched examples, to categorize such accredited routes to knowledge, even though the attempts have been, wrongly in my opinion, viewed only as giving criteria for the justified true belief of a claimant to knowledge. I shall not examine these attempts, since I believe that in practice we commonly allow a good deal more flexibility and latitude in the attribution of knowledge than such attempts envisage or permit. Moreover, such questions relate to the application of the concept of knowledge rather than to its nature. In fact, if someone is in touch with reality, we usually allow that he knows unless either we are puzzled as to how he could have managed it or some suggestion that it was chance is actually made.

CHAPTER FIVE

Theories of Knowledge

There have in the history of philosophy been at least half a dozen different theories of the nature of knowledge, that is, answers to the question "What is knowledge?." Each can be regarded, illuminatingly I think, though without any historical authenticity, as an attempt to model the verb "know," or its equivalent in other languages, on some other class of verbs. Thus, "to know" is said (a) to express a mental *act* analogously to the way in which, e.g., "to speak" or "to walk" expresses a physical act; (b) to express a mental *achievement* in the way in which, e.g., "to hit" or "to win" expresses a physical achievement; (c) to express a mental *state* or *condition,* such as "to be certain" or "to be sure," in the way that "to be stable" or "to be rotten" expresses a physical state; (d) to express, at least in its first person singular present tense, a mental *performance,* as "to christen" or "to salute" expresses a physical performance; (e) to express a mental *disposition,* whether a *tendency* or a *liability,* as "to conduct electricity" or "to hibernate" expresses a physical disposition; or (f) to express a mental ability, as "to hold water" expresses a physical ability.

Let us, therefore, consider in turn each of these attempted analyses of *knowledge,* bearing in mind, as we have seen, that such knowledge includes knowing what, when, where, who or how A V's or to V, knowing the colour or size of something, knowing French, knowing that p and knowing people, places and conditions.

A. KNOWLEDGE AS ACTION

Because verbs are very commonly used to indicate some act which people perform or some activity in which they engage, such as striking or sawing, whistling or speaking, philosophers have traditionally assumed that "know" is also used like this; especially, that it is used to refer to a mental act. Thus, Descartes[1] said that "the act of mind by which a thing is believed is different from that by which we know that we believe it" and Locke[2] spoke of "that action which they call knowing." This tradition lingers on in some contemporary philosophical writing.[3] It may also be at the root of the old controversy between Idealist and Realist philosophers whether knowing affects the thing known as, e.g., hitting affects the thing hit. The alleged analogy between knowing and acting may also be partly responsible for too literal a picture of what is known as the "object" of knowledge in the way that what is hit is the "object" hit.

The concept of knowledge, however, lacks the usual characteristics of action concepts. It makes no sense to speak of someone's being interrupted or uninterrupted while knowing the date of the battle of Waterloo or while knowing how to do quadratic equations. We cannot spend all morning or even a split second knowing anything. Knowing is not something we do quickly or slowly, carefully or haphazardly, deliberately or impulsively. The continuous forms "I am knowing" and "He was knowing" are solecisms of syntax peculiar to philosophers. Nor can I be caught in the act of knowing. I cannot resolve, promise or refuse to know; I cannot compel or cajole anyone into knowing. I do not cease to know while my mind is actually engaged in doing other things, such as puzzling, reminiscing, worrying or sleeping. Nor do I have to think of, or give my attention to, something in order at any moment to know it.

B. KNOWLEDGE AS ACHIEVEMENT

As a matter of grammar the English verb "to know" can, perhaps, sometimes be used to refer to an acquisition or attainment. We can ask the detective when did he first know that the butler was an ex-convict; we can tell someone that we did not know until last night that we would not be able to attend the meeting. Similarly, we can say both that someone "got" sixpence on his birthday and that he has now "got" sixpence. Asking a person how he knew so and so is often a request for the means by which he got access to it. But it is clear that "know" is used in these examples as an idiomatic short form for "get to or come to know," "discover," etc. And "getting to know" something is logically different from "knowing" it. We ask someone when did he get to know, but how long he has known, a date, the alphabet or a colleague. Our means and methods of acquiring knowledge may be devious or debatable, but there are no means or methods of having knowledge. Getting to know the time of a meeting or the hang of an argument is something we may try for a long time and at which we may, suddenly or gradually, succeed or fail; but knowing the time is not something we can try or succeed or fail in. Possession implies and is implied by acquisition, but to acquire anything, including knowledge, is not the same as possessing it. "Realise" is also commonly used analogously both for "get to know" and for "know."

It is sometimes suggested[4] that Gilbert Ryle considered "know" an *achievement* or *got it* verb, that is, as signifying "not only that some performance has been gone through, but also that something has been brought off by the agent going through it."[5] And certainly much of what Ryle says about knowing something does imply or even express this view. First, he groups (pp. 130, 152–3, 239) "know" with such verbs as "find," "discover," "prove," "solve," "see," "detect," "deduce," "recall," "conclude," all of which latter he rightly holds are achievements or, perhaps better, acquisitions.

Secondly, he sometimes (e.g., pp. 150–1) moves from the view that achievement verbs "signify not only that some performance has been gone through but also that something has been brought off by the agent going through it" to the view that "in applying an achievement verb we are asserting that some state of affairs obtains over and above that which consists in the performance, if any, of the subservient task activity." Thirdly, he sometimes groups "being right," which is a characteristic of knowing, that is, the possession of knowledge, with "succeeding," which is not. Fourthly, he overlooks (pp. 239, 134) the fact that the question "How do you know?" can be used either, and perhaps more commonly, to ask how someone got hold of his knowledge or to ask him how it is that he possesses that knowledge. And, hence, fifthly, much of his discussion (e.g., pp. 40–1) of how one acquires either knowledge of how to do something or the ability to do it does not distinguish it from the possession of that know-how, or that ability.

In so far as Ryle does undoubtedly say these things, he is wrong. He has rightly distinguished both "discover," "solve," "detect," etc., and "know" from "search," "puzzle over," "look for," etc.; but wrongly concluded that "know" is to be contrasted in the same way with these latter as is "detect," "solve," "discover."

To know, as we have just seen, is not to achieve something; it is to possess it, even if the verb "know" in English is sometimes used as an abbreviation for "get to know." Yet all of Ryle's arguments above assimilate knowing, that is possessing knowledge, to achieving or acquiring knowledge. "Know" is not in fact in the same class as "discover," "prove," "solve," "detect," "deduce" or "conclude." Though one can get to know something, as one can discover, prove or solve it, at a particular point in time, one knows something for or during a particular time. One can know something for years, but not get to know, solve or discover it for years. On the other hand, whereas one can take years to solve, discover or get to know something, one cannot take years to know it. One can forget how to discover, prove or solve something, but not forget how to know it; though one can, of course, forget the thing itself. "Knowing," unlike "discovering," "proving" and "solving," does not signify "that something has been brought off," but that "some state of affairs obtains over and above" either a corresponding task or a corresponding achievement. "Succeeding" is not "being right,' though success in certain tasks may result in being right. One can know well or better, thoroughly, off by heart, etc., but not discover, prove, detect or come to know in these ways. One can have the ability to solve, discover or prove something, but not the ability to know it. Abilities, but not achievements, can be built up by practice. And one can put into practice one's abilities or one's knowledge, but not one's achievements. "Knowing," i.e., having knowledge, is no more the same as "coming to know," i.e., achieving or acquiring knowledge, than "being President" is the same as "becoming President" or "being at the airport" is the same as "arriving at the airport."

Ryle's real or apparent adherence to an achievement view of the use of the verb "know" is, moreover, inconsistent with much of what he says about knowing in other parts of, e.g., *The Concept of Mind*. For there (e.g., pp., 44–6, 59, 133) he undoubtedly argues, not that "know" signifies an achievement, but that it signifies a possession, namely, the possesion of a disposition or, rather, an ability or a capacity. Significantly, the index to the *Concept of Mind* refers under "know" not to the idea of an achievement, but to those of a disposition and a capacity. "Know" is said to signify a capacity to "bring things off" or "get them right," not simply "bringing them off" or "getting them right" themselves. Nor is a capacity or a disposition to achieve a type of achievement, e.g., "a capacity achievement,"[6] anymore than a capacity or a disposition to act or suffer is a type of act or a type of suffering. To prove or to detect are achievements, whereas the ability or capacity to prove or to detect, though they may be capacities to achieve are not themselves achievements; yet it is with "prove" and "detect" that Ryle earlier compared "know." Certain tasks may enable one to achieve what one is after, whether it is knoweldge or some other prize, but what one does achieve is not itself an achievement. "Knowing" may pre-suppose "having learnt," but it is not equivalent to it (cp. p. 226). Nor is the distinction between an achievement and a possession confined by Ryle to knowing how to do something, for he also says that knowing that something is so is to have and retain a store-house of truths, not that it is the acquisition of such a store-house. Furthermore, Ryle himself emphasises in another context (pp. 301–3) the difference between, e.g., having a plan, an argument or a proof and getting any of these; and in his *Dilemmas*[7] he recognises that, e.g., "discovering" is "coming to know" and not "knowing,"[8] even though one obviously knows that which one has come to know.

Hence, I conclude, first, that Ryle wavered between viewing "know" as a verb expressing the achievement of something and viewing it as a verb expressing the possession of it; and, secondly, that the former view is mistaken.

C. KNOWLEDGE AS STATE

The theory that to know something is to be in a certain state or condition of mind has been very popular in the philosophical tradition.[9] Knowledge, however, is very different from anything, such as worry, indecision, confidence, hope or joy, which would ordinarily be called a state or condition of mind. It is arguable, for instance, that there is only a slight, if any, difference between "being" worried or confident, undecided or in despair, and "feeling" any of these. Could someone feel confident or hopeful and yet not be so? But to feel that you know the answer to an examination question is only too frequently compatible with your not knowing it at all. Similarly, as Wittgenstein once emphasised,[10] "doubt, belief, certainty—like feelings, emotions, pain, etc.—have characteristic facial expressions. Knowledge does *not* have a characteristic facial expression. There is a *tone* of doubt, and a tone of conviction, but no tone of knowledge." If a man gave me a "knowing look," he would think he knew but might not know. In "He looks as if he knew" or "He sounds as if he knew," the looks and sounds do not refer to facial features and tones, but to ways of behaviour, e.g., competence, skill, grasp of intricacies, surefootedness, which suggest knowledge. Our worry or confidence, our indecision or hope, may be faint or deeprooted, but these are not characteristics of our knowledge. If my knowledge is greater than yours, then I know more things or know them more thoroughly than you; but if my anxiety or hope is greater than yours, I am more deeply affected by them. Again, we have various means, from propaganda to auto-suggestion, of inducing states of mind in others and in ourselves, and we can disturb a man's peace of mind or shake his confidence; but to inform or misinform someone is not to induce a state of mind, nor is raising an objection to disturb his knowledge. We can ask *why* someone is confident or feels confident as we ask why he is worried or happy, but we cannot ask why he knows. Contrariwise, we may enquire *how* he knows, but not how he is confident, worried or happy. We can, perhaps, teach the meaning of words for states of minds ostensively, that is, by using the appropriate word to describe the state in which the pupil is now. But the meaning of the word "knowledge" cannot be taught like this, for it has a reference to something other than the state of the person who claims to know.

The methods of discovering whether someone is in a certain state of mind differ importantly from the methods of discovering whether he knows so and so.[11] First of all, it makes no difference to our attempts to discover whether a student really knows or only thinks he knows the date of the battle or how to extract square roots that sometimes the student is oneself and sometimes he is another; but finding out whether someone sincerely thinks he knows or is only bluffing, like finding out whether he is pretending to be cheerful or really is cheerful, has special difficulties when the candidate is someone other than ourselves. It is equally possible to wonder whether we ourselves know or whether another knows, but whereas we may often be in doubt whether another feels undecided or depressed, we cannot doubt whether we feel undecided or depressed. "I think I know" makes sense where "I think I am undecided" does not. There is some plausibility in the supposition that one can find out whether he himself is confident or anxious by examining, perhaps introspectively, his own state of mind, but it is simply a mistake to say[12] that introspection could show anyone whether he knows the names of all the Derby winners or only believes he does. The state of mind of a man who sincerely, but mistakenly, thinks he knows something need be no different from that of someone who does know it; and even where it is different, this provides not the slightest clue to his knowledge or lack of knowledge. A particular state of mind, such as confidence or depression, hope or fear, may be warranted or unwarranted by the facts of the situation, but knowledge cannot be unwarranted.

If, then, knowledge is not, in any ordinary sense, a state or condition of mind, why has this mistaken view seemed so plausible? The main reason is probably a confusion of knowledge with confidence and certainy. Philosophers[13] have sometimes argued that "in certain uses of these terms, and these perfectly legitimate uses, 'feeling sure' and 'knowing' are synonymous." Now, if this were true, knowledge might legitimately be called a state of mind, for confidence has the characteristics of a state of mind. For instance, it is something which can be felt, which can be expressed in one's face and in one's manner and which can in various degrees and by various means be induced in oneself or in another. It is something which one discovers in another by watching his behaviour and which one may perhaps discover in oneself introspectively. It may be justified or unjustified. But we have just seen that none of this is true of knowledge. What has misled philosophers into the assimilation of knowledge and confidence is the fact that commonly one *says* "I know" when and only when one is confident. To say "I know" is often to put forward a claim; and since we do not sincerely and justifiably put forward claims to knowledge or to anything else, unless we feel confident of their validity, it follows that whenever we are prepared to say "I know" we do feel (or pretend to feel) very confident, and usually *vice versa*. A man shows—though he does not describe—his confidence by his willingness to claim to know, by his saying "I know." But a man may feel confident, say "I know," and yet not really know at all. Not all claims are valid. Confidence, but not knowledge, can be misplaced. Yet to show that someone's confidence is misplaced, that he does not in fact know what he claims to know, is not to show that he was not confident or that he was not justified in expressing his confidence by saying "I know."

A second possible reason for the thesis that knowledge is a state of mind may be an adherence to the view that where there is knowledge of something there is also belief in it, together with the not implausible theory that belief at least is a state of mind. Most attempts, from Plato onwards, to provide criteria for knowledge have, as we saw, consisted in the search for requirements, restrictions and restraints—such as truth or justification—on a central core of belief or certainty. They have proceeded on the assumption that belief is one state of mind and knowledge another and that the latter is a species of which the former is the genus.

A third possible reason for the thesis may be an undue reliance on the use of "know" in cases of indecision. To characterise the man who, faced with the problem of deciding on a course of action, cannot make up his mind what to do, as "not knowing what to do" is to link his knowledge to the state which he is in. Hence, "I thought I knew what to call my dog" is queer in a way that "I thought I knew the date of Easter" or "I thought I knew how to extract square roots" are not. A man can tell by self-examination whether his mind is made up or whether he is still undecided, but he cannot tell in this way whether he knows the date of Easter, but only whether he is confident about it. The main difference between the man who knows where he is going to spend his holidays and the man who does not is a state of mind, but the main difference between a man who knows where to find the missing key and one who does not is a difference in the information held. Nevertheless, as we saw, whether the reason why one does not know what to do or where to go is either that there is an answer to that question which one cannot find or that one cannot decide what the answer shall be, the lack of knowledge is the same thing.

D. KNOWLEDGE AS PERFORMANCE

Many verbs are clearly used, in the first person singular, present indicative, to *say* what the user of the verb is doing. Thus, to say "I twist," "I turn" or "I lift" is to *say* what I am doing; it is certainly not to *do* it.

J. L. Austin recently[14] drew the attention of philosophers to the fact that some verbs, in their first person singular, present indicative, are, on the other hand, perhaps primarily used *to do* something rather than *to say* what one is doing. Thus, to say, in appropriate circumstances, "I promise," "I warn" or "I baptise" is to promise, to warn or to baptise rather than, or at least as well as, to say that I am promising, warning or baptising. It is to perform rather than, or at least as well as, to describe. Unfortunately, by comparing "I know" with the latter verbs, Austin gave the impression that he thought that to say "I know" is not, primarily at least, to say that I know or, in his words, "to say that I have performed a specially striking feat of cognition;" it is to do something.

Clearly, however, what, if anything, I do by saying "I know" is not—as he expressly admitted—to know, in the way that what I do by saying "I promise" or "I warn" is to promise or to warn; nor, of course, is it actually to perform a specially striking feat of cognition. Though saying "I promise" or "I warn" is one way of promising or warning, saying "I know" is not a way of knowing. At most it is, as he alleged, to give others my word, to give others my authority; thought it is not, in fact, just to do one thing. It can be used to claim, admit, concede, etc., that one knows, as well, of course, as to say that I know. Indeed, we have already seen the often overlooked contrast between one of the things that saying "I know" does, namely, to claim to know, and knowing itself. Austin was in fact falling into the common trap of shifting his analysis from knowledge to claims to knowledge. Similarly, to say of someone else "He knew" is not to report something he did—either to know or to give his word—when he said "I know" in the way that to say of him "He promised" is to report something he did—namely, to promise—when he said "I promise." Someone who says "I promise" has promised, however things turn out. What someone who says "I knew" has done, however things turn out, is not to know, but only to claim to know. Grammatically, a man who last week said "I promise" is reported this week as having promised ("You promised"), whereas a man who last week said "I know" is reported this week not as having known ("You knew"), but as having said he knew ("You claimed to know"). Hence, we can, and commonly do, reply to someone who says "I know" by remarking "You said you knew, but you don't (or didn't)," whereas we can't reply to someone who says "I promise" by remarking "You said you promised, but you don't (or didn't)." Further, even if to say "I know" were to do something rather than to say or describe what I was doing, as to say "I promise" is to promise rather than to say that I am promising, the former would throw no more light on what it is to know something than the latter throws light on what it is to promise something. There is, in fact, no incompatibility between using the first person singular present indicative of the verb to do so and so and using it to say what one is doing or even to say something else.[15] Thus, to say "I am warning you that if you do that again, you will be sacked" may be both to warn and to say that you are warning. To say "There's a bull in that field" may be both to warn and to say something about the field. What is important for us is to discover what one is either doing or saying that one is doing when one says "I know" or "I promise," "I warn" or "I baptise," etc.

No theory of the nature of knowledge could rest on the alleged performative use of "know," which is confined to the first person present indicative, "I know," since what it is to know anything will be the same whether it is something I know, he knows, I knew or they will know.

Further, Austin's particular suggestion that what I do when I say "I know" is to give others my word or to give others my authority for saying something is at most only plausible for "I know that p." One can talk about giving one's word or one's authority for saying that p. But what would one be giving others one's word about or what would one be giving others one's authority for saying in "I know what, where, how A V's," "I know what, where, how to V," "I know the result, or the name, of X," "I know Paris," or "I know the Director of Education?" It would not be sufficient for Austin's thesis merely to answer that one was giving one's word or one's authority for saying that one knew those. And it would make no sense to say that one was giving one's word or one's authority for saying what, where or how A V's, where or how to V, the result or name of X, Paris or the Director of Education.

E. KNOWLEDGE AS DISPOSITION

i. Many of the concepts we use to describe the mental and moral characteristics of men are of a *tendency* kind; that is, they refer to the sorts of things which men frequently or commonly do and achieve rather than to the particular things which they are actually doing or have just achieved or to the state they are now in. Traits, like vanity, indolence, conceit, timidity, generosity or honesty, as well as habits, such as stroking one's chin, tidying up one's desk each evening or checking one's answers, are signified by tendency concepts. Is knowledge of this kind? Certainly, it resembles a tendency in not being like an activity or achievement or state of mind. Further, knowledge, like a habit, is something we can acquire, retain and lose. Like a habit, it is not something that takes time to do, nor something we can be interrupted in. The most fruitful result of comparing knowledge with any disposition is that it enables us to see how knowledge can be something we possess and yet not something for which we have to find a storehouse or receptacle; and, therefore, how we can escape the conclusion that our minds must be rather mysterious storehouses. For it is easy to see that a man who has certain tendencies, certain traits and habits, does not have certain entities which he needs to store away when he is not showing them. There is no answer to the question "Where is my conceit when I am not displaying it?." Hiding one's envy is not like hiding one's ear-rings. My habit, long ago acquired, of taking a nap after dinner, does not disappear when I am not indulging in it, nor yet is there a place where it is kept.

Nevertheless, it is clear that knowledge is not a tendency; it is very unlike a habit or a trait. Tendencies are linked to frequencies of behaviour. One could not have a habit which one never or hardly ever exhibited, and an increase in a tendency is an increase in the occasions of its manifestations. Our knowledge, however, need never be revealed; and an increase in it is an increase in the amount we have acquired, not in the occasions on which we display it. Nor is knowledge usually acquired or lost in the way that habits and traits are acquired and lost.

ii. Another type of dispositional concept common in the description of human and other characteristics is that of a *liability*. These concepts are sometimes assimilated to tendency concepts, with which they have many characteristics in common. Neither refers to anything actually happening at the moment, but to something which may be acquired, retained and lost, yet needs no place to be stored in when not manifested. Nevertheless, liabilities are different from tendencies. To say of someone that he does so and so *whenever* such and such happens (that is, has a tendency) is not the same as saying that he would do so and so *if* ever such and such happened (that is, has a liability). The second follows from the first, though not the first from the second. What tends to happen must frequently happen, whereas what is liable to happen may, fortunately or unfortunately, never happen because the conditions of its happening never crop up. My initial complaint that the new clock is so delicate that it is *liable* to go wrong is logically different from my later complaint that it *tends* to go wrong. A common reason for assimilating the concepts is that our evidence for saying that someone or something is liable to do so and so, such as fly off the handle, is normally either his or its having a tendency to do it or being of a species that has such a tendency. A weak-willed fellow is liable to give in to temptation, though he may luckily have never been tempted.

But knowledge is no more a liability than a tendency. The man who knows something need neither tend to do anything nor be liable to. Whereas I could not be properly described as amiable or irascible unless I acted in an amiable or irascible way in certain conditions, it is not self-contradictory to say that someone knows something even though in all conditions he refrains from showing it. A man who knows the date of the battle of the Boyne or how to tie a reef-knot need not be liable to show this knowledge when the occasion warrants. Moreover, liabilities are usually defects. Just as an unstable mixture is liable to blow up or break down, so a man who lacks the requisite knowledge is liable to get the answer wrong.

F. KNOWLEDGE AS ABILITY

Resembling both tendency and liability concepts are those which signify an ability. Abilities, like tendencies, are not activities in which we engage nor processes which go on in us; to be able to do something is not to be in a state of mind, nor is having an ability possessing an entity of some sort. It makes no sense to ask where an ability is between the time we acquire it and the time we lose it. To suppose that abilities must be stored somewhere is to confuse them with the physical mechanisms that make their operation possible. But a man no more has abilities in his mind in the way that he has layers in his brain than a car has the capacity to do 100 m.p.h. under its bonnet in the way that it has pistons in its cylinders.

Abilities, however, differ from tendencies and liabilities in that they involve neither a frequent nor a conditional performance of any kind. One need have no tendency to use the abilities one has, nor is it at all self-contradictory to say that one is able to do something which, whatever the circumstances, one would never do. Most people are, no doubt, able to say every fifth letter of the alphabet, but this is not something that they either tend to do, nor in any circumstances are necessarily liable to do. Perhaps the most important way in which an ability or capacity differs from a tendency and a liability is that the former notion has the idea of success or achievement built into it. One may tend or be liable either to do or to suffer something, such as stroking one's chin or getting into a rage, in which no question of success or failure arises; but we speak of abilities only where there is the idea of a standard which could be reached. Thus, we do not say that a man is able to become depressed or to grow pale. It is as possible to tend to or be liable to fail as it is to succeed; but while hitting the target is something we may or may not be able to do, we would not call missing it four out of every five times an ability, unless we were trying to miss it.

Is to say that someone knows so and so to say that he has a certain ability? The possession of knowledge, like the possession of an ability, is not inconsistent with its never being used or revealed. There is a time when the knowledge or ability was acquired, there may be a time when they are lost and there is a time during which they are possessed. But the man who possesses them need be doing nothing, either now or occasionally, while he has them; nor need he keep them anywhere. If a man possesses something, he has not lost it and can, in principle at least, produce it. If a man knows something, he has not forgotten it and can, therefore, display it. It might be generally admitted that a man who has knowledge of something is able to produce this knowledge just as a man who has a railway ticket is able to produce it. But then, it might be said, there is a difference between having something and being able to produce it. The latter is only a consequence of the former; we could not produce something unless we already had it somewhere. Isn't it because we already have our knowledge stored somewhere, say in our mind or in our memory, that we are able to produce it on demand? The answer to this objection, as we have hinted, is that not everything that can be produced is some kind of entity which must have existed somewhere before its production. All that we need have is the ability to produce it; and abilities are not located anywhere. For instance, the smile I produce on hearing good news, the display of strength I produce to frighten my opponent, the clever tactics I display when cornered, do not exist before their production; all that I need in order to produce them is the ability to produce them.

It might be conceded that this reply is plausible enough where one's knowledge is how, where, when, et cetera to do something of a certain sort, such as how to ride a bicycle, where to put the accent on Spanish words or when to add to the mixture in a certain process, because here the relevant abilities are not merely to produce old answers previously acquired, but to find new answers to new problems. In attributing knowledge that p, however, it might be objected that we must distinguish between the possession of that knowledge and the ability to produce it, which is only the evidence that we have it, since what is required here are only learnt and stored answers to the same old problems. Moreover, certain common idioms of our talk about such informational knowledge seem, at first sight, to support this objection; an objection which Wittgenstein characterised as the assumption that "Knowledge is the hypothesized reservoir out of which the visible water flows."[16]

Information is said to be fed into us or lapped up by us and given out again in much the same form; therefore, the exhibition of such knowledge must be a literal production of it from where it was stored. In general we acquire knowledge of facts and truths by amassing, filing away, swallowing, stuffing ourselves with, various details. The human encyclopaedia is a man stored and stuffed with information. Further, we idiomatically speak of our head or brain or mind or memory as the place where we store these facts, as the receptacle that is stuffed with or full of them. We distinguish between the man who fills his drawers, his bookshelves and his filing cabinets with the information he has gathered and the man who keeps it all in his head. To know the details of the Korean war or the names of the presidents of the United States, it might be said, is to have this information packed away inside us, readily— or, if we have untidy minds, not so readily—available for production on request.

Certainly, these are the idioms in which we talk of knowledge of facts, of the possession of information. But are they to be taken literally, as this picture of knowledge suggests, or are they metaphors drawn by analogy from the literal ways in which we store such physical objects as papers, books, files and record cards? First, facts, truths, ideas, statements, are not sorts of entities. To discover a few new facts about a murder is not like discovering a few extra bloodstains and footprints, though it may be that in discovering the bloodstains and footprints the detective has thereby discovered the new facts. Nor when he files away the facts in his mind to be examined at leisure does he literally wrap them up in immaterial envelopes and put them in immaterial pigeon-holes as he does with the material bloodstains and the plaster casts of the footprints which he posts off to the forensic laboratory. The man who "discovers" the truth, "acquires" information, "gets hold of" the facts, like the man who "grasps" an idea, "examines" a theory, is not dealing in exactly the same way—that is discovering, acquiring, grasping, etc.,—with mental or abstract entities called "truths," "facts," etc., as the man who discovers water, acquires a new car, gets hold of the end of a stick, is dealing with physical entities; it is the dealings of the former which are different from, though analogous to, the dealings of the latter. In other words, it must not be assumed that the only difference in meaning between "acquiring X" and "acquiring Y" lies in the difference in meaning of "X" and "Y" and that, therefore, everything which is acquired must be kept *somewhere*, however different the sorts of places in which they are kept.

Even the analogy between keeping information "in our head" and keeping it in our filing cabinet does not show what it is often thought to show. If a Secret Service file contains all the details of my early life, it also contains various ink-marks on paper. The marks on paper are not the details of my life; to destroy these marks might deprive the Secret Service of the details but it would not destroy the details. Yet there is not a special non-material compartment in the file for keeping the details as well as the ink marks. Similarly, if a Secret Service agent has those details in his head, the details are not any marks on his brain, which may, for all I know, normally result from his committing the details to memory, nor yet is there a special non-material compartment in his head for keeping the details. Further, just as the details contained in the file need not be reproduced from it in the exact (verbal) form in which they were entered, so the agent need not reproduce the information he has acquired in the form in which he acquired it. Reproducing the information of the file is not reproducing the marks on paper, nor is reproducing the information of the agent reproducing either the marks on his brain nor the words he read or heard when he acquired the information. Take another analogy. Suppose we have a musical box which plays "Holy Night." In what sense must the box contain or have this tune inside it in order that it should reproduce it on demand? Well, it must be able to, have the capacity to, produce the tune. But no-one supposes that either the capacity to produce the tune or the actual tune lies anywhere under the lid. What does lie under the lid is the mechanism—perhaps certain metal, clockwork pieces arranged in a certain order—which gives the box the capacity to produce the tune. But these metal pieces are not the tune; they are neither loud nor soft, sweet nor harsh, reminiscent of our choirboy days nor attributable to an early German poet. Similarly, neither Leibniz's *Monadology* nor the date of his birth, which I now know pretty well, nor my ability to enunciate these or correct the enunciations of others is in my brain or anywhere else. Nor can the brain mechanisms which enable me to make my enunciations and correct those of others be called Leibniz's theory or the date of his birth. The mechanisms, unlike the theory, are not the result of Leibniz's work on mathematics; philosophers do not write commentaries on these mechanisms; if I forget or make mistakes in the theory, I do not forget or make mistakes in the mechanisms. To say that the theories are now in my head and not merely in my books, that is, that I have at last mastered them, is to say that I can now propound them without the help of the books.

Although, in many cases, we can distinguish between acquiring something, e.g., a letter, and acquiring the ability to produce it—the former being an indispensable cause of the latter—in other cases to acquire something is to acquire the ability to produce it.

The ability in which knowledge consists differs from other abilities, e.g., the ability to hold six pints of liquid in one's stomach or sixteen digits in one's head, in that it is the ability to produce the correct answer to a possible question, the solution of a possible problem. This is most obvious where our knowledge is expressed by "know" and an interrogative. To know what, where, when or how to V or what, where, when or how A V's—or the thing, place, time or way either to V or which A V's—is to be able to produce, in word or action, the answers to the questions introduced by these interrogatives. Similarly, since knowing a characteristic of something, e.g., its weight, colour or shape, is, as we saw, knowing what is this characteristic and knowing, e.g., French or one's twelve times tables is knowing how to do something, here also there is a question whose answer the person who knows is able to supply. Equally, to know that p is to be able to give an answer, namely that p, which is in fact the correct answer to a possible question. Nor is knowledge of people, places or conditions, e.g., of Paris, Queen Elizabeth or poverty, any exception to this. For we saw that to know these is to know something about them through having had direct experience of them. It is what we know about them, not they themselves, which constitute the "object" of our knowledge. And this knowledge, like the rest of our knowledge, is the ability to produce the correct answers to questions about them. The greater this ability, the greater our degree of knowledge of them, whether it be barely, scarcely, slightly, well, intimately, inside out or like the back of one's hand.

That one has the ability to produce the required answer in any of these cases may be manifested by showing it or telling it, by deed or word, directly or indirectly. For example, one may show that one knows the murderer, that is, knows who is the murderer, by pointing to him, by distinguishing between alternative suggestions about his identity or by picking him out in an identification parade. Sometimes we might insist that a man be able to indicate, recognise and distinguish the right answer to a question before he be admitted to know the truth; but often we do not insist that a failure only to indicate the answer precludes knowledge of it. Some people are verbally inarticulate and all of us find it easier to recognise, e.g., the German word for "knife" when we see or hear it than to say what it is, if asked. Recognising faces we know is often easier than recalling names we know. We can rightly be said to know what a violin sounds like or what salted peanuts taste like without being able to describe or reproduce the taste or sound, if we can distinguish such sounds and tastes from others.

To know "The Ancient Mariner" might consist in one's ability to recite passages of it, to supply missing words, to correct misquotations, etc., and to know that Leibniz was born in 1646 might consist in the ability to give that date, to distinguish it from other proffered dates, to link it correctly with the date of Berkeley's birth, etc.

To know a person or place is at least to be able to indicate, recognise and distinguish who or what it is. But since people, places and productions are also complexes or structures of one kind or another, to know them is also to be able to tell about their composition and make up. To know a person is to be able to tell his character, his opinions, his attitudes. A knowledgeable wife can tell almost exactly what her husband thinks or would think, how he will react to so and so, whether he will be pleased or displeased about, agree or object to such and such. A man may know his native town inside out, in every nook and cranny, every twist and bend. A critic may get to know his author's work like its own creator who fashioned it, in every limb and joint. When a man dies and when a place or a production is destroyed, we can only say that we knew them, not that we still know them since there is now no structure within whose intricacies we can any longer find or lose our way.

Furthermore, since the ability to provide the right answer to a possible question implies neither knowing that one has this ability nor manifesting it in any verbal way, there is no reason why young children and animals should not be said to know many things, whether it be, e.g., how to open a door, where to go for food, what shape or size something is, that it is time for a walk, or their favourite people and places.

Notes

CHAPTER ONE

1. Griffiths, 1967, 1; cp. Hamlyn, 1970, 5; Ayer, 1956, 32, 34, 71, etc; Ackermann, 1972, 55, 60, 64–7; Rynin, 1967, 29; Evans, 1978, 38, 45, 106, 109, 121, 130–1, 137, etc, though contrast 116, 118; Danto, 1968, takes a rather ambivalent position in ch. 1, but in the rest of the book analyses claims to knowledge.
2. Lehrer, 1974.
3. Hintikka, 1962, esp. chs. 4 and 5.
4. Pollock, 1974, 5–my italics.
5. Munsat, 1966, 65, 123, ch. IV *passim;* but contrast 83, 123.
6. Cp. Danto, 1968, 26 fl.; Lehrer, 1974, chs. 1 and 3.
7. E.g., Austin 1946; Hamlyn, 1970, 102; Carl and Horstmann, 1972.
8. White, 1957, reprinted in Griffiths 1967, 111; Warnock, 1962, 19–32.
9. E.g. Rynin, 1967, 10; Carl and Horstmann, 1972; Butchvarov, 1970, 89 and *passim,* holds that "I know that p" is equivalent to "I find it unthinkable that I am mistaken in believing that p;" cp. Ackermann, 1972, 67, 75–6.
10. Austin, 1946, 148 fl.
11. It is significant that Warnock's acceptance, 1962, 25–6, of justified confidence as a necessary condition for knowledge goes with his denial of the relevance of an investigation into the logic of claims to an enquiry about the nature of knowledge.
12. E.g., Lehrer, 1974, and Pollock, 1974.
13. E.g., Prichard, 1950, reprinted in Griffiths 1967, 88; Griffiths 1967, 61; Armstrong, J.H.S., 1953, 117.
14. E.g., contrast Malcolm, 1952, reprinted in Griffiths 1967, 69 fl. with 1954, 87.
15. E.g., Armstrong, D.M. 1972, 216.
16. E.g., Malcolm, 1976, 216–40; Wolgast, 1978, Ch. III.
17. E.g., Carl and Horstmann, 1972, 159–61, who miss the difference between "He is correct (right) in saying that p" and "What he said, namely that p, is correct (right)."
18. E.g., Aaron, 1956, 2, 10, 12.

CHAPTER TWO

1. Woozley, 1953, reprinted in Griffiths, 1967, 94–5, would have to deny this, since he holds that "knowing that" implies, whereas "knowing what, where, etc.," does not, that one is able to show that one's answer is right.
2. This has to be read as "There is a place, time etc., of which A knows that it is the place, time . . ." and not as "A knows that X is the place, time, etc. . . . ," since "X" may be a description of the place, time, etc., under which A does not know that it is the place, time, etc., ...
3. Woozley, 1953, 86–8, alleges that "know how to" followed by an achievement verb does imply "knowing that," whereas "know how to" followed by a task verb

124 NOTES

does not. This is because he takes "know how to" in the former, but not in the latter, to involve knowing the preliminary process necessary to achieve the result. But what we know, whenever we know how to, is the *way* to V.

4. Ryle, 1946, 1–16.

5. Ryle, 1949, ch. 2.

6. The thesis seems to be accepted by, e.g., Geach, 1977, 21–2; though he thinks this "can" is different from that of physical power; cp. von Wright, 1963, 48.

7. This is quite different from the thesis of Carr, 1979, 409, that "reports of knowing how differ from those of ability in taking members of a different class of action descriptions for their objects. . . . those of intentional actions rather than mere instances of agent-causation." This thesis is based on the premiss that "know how" is unlike "able to" in that if A knows how to V and to V is to F, it does not follow that A knows how to F. But this premiss depends for its plausibility on the false assumption that one cannot know how to V without knowing that one knows how to V.

8. as Scheffler, 1965, 93–4, seems to do.

9. Brown, 1970, 213–48; cp. Cohen, 1962, 50; Woozley, 1953, 86–8, alleges several ambiguities in "know how," including one sense which is equivalent to a learnt ability and one which is not, and one which takes "task" verbs and one which takes "achievement" verbs; Carr, 1979, 394–409, on the other hand, seems to suppose there are various senses of "can," of which one is "physical ability" and another "know how."

10. E.g., Gould, 1955, Ch. I.

11. E.g., some Greek commentators cited by Gould, 1955. For details on Greek verbs of knowing, see Snell, 1924.

12. Cp. note 3 above.

13. P. 223; cp. 239.

14. Brett, 1974, 293–300.

15. Brown, 1974, 301–3.

16. E.g., Brown, 1970, 1974, and Danto, 1968, 20–1; Evans, 1978, 4, 83–5.

17. Ryle, 1946, 4, 7–9.

18. Ryle, 1949, 41; contrast 55.

19. *Pace* Brett, 1974, 299.

20. This also underlies Scheffler's, 1965, Ch 5, assimilation of knowing how and skill.

21. Cp. Brett, 1974, 299–300; Evans, 1978, 84.

22. Russell, 1912, 73.

23. *Phaedo,* 74b2

24. Cp. Scheffler, 1965, 7.

25. *Meno,* 87c2; cp. Barnes, J, 1980, 196.

26. Cp. Austin, 1946.

27. E.g., Hamlyn, 1970, 101; Harrison, 1962, reprinted in Griffiths, 1967, 114; Klein, 1971, 471–82; Chisholm, 1976, 1–20; Evans, 1978, 17 fl., 37, 44, 51, 54, 56, etc.

28. E.g., Hamlyn, 1970, ch. 4, § 6; Braithwaite, 1933, 129–46; Chisholm, 1976.

29. E.g., Ayer, 1956, Ch.I; Hamlyn, 1970, 101; Margolis, 1973, 19; cp. Locke, *Essay,* IV. i. 8 fl., Chisholm, 1976; Evans, 1978, 22–3, 26, 52.

30. E.g., Ayer, 1956.

31. E.g., Russell, 1940, 171, cp. 62, 155, 189; Mayo, 1964, reprinted in Griffiths, 1967, 147.

32. Cp. White, 1972; Prior, 1971, 14–16.

33. Cp. Danto, 1968, Ch. 4.
34. Cp. my "Knowledge, Acquaintance and Awareness" *Midwest Studies in Philosophy*, 6, (1981) 159–72, edited by French, Wettstein and Uehling.

CHAPTER THREE

1. 476 fl; cp. *Republic*, VI, *Timaeus*, 28, 51–2; *Philebus*, 58–9.
2. E.g., *Post Analytics*, 88b–89b.
3. Price, 1935.
4. Vendler, 1972.
5. Cp. *Republic*, 510.
6. White, 1974a, 1974b.
7. Jones, 1975.
8. Dunn and Suter, 1977.
9. *Republic*, 476 fl.
10. Vendler, 1978.
11. This seems to be all that Kiparsky and Kiparsky, 1971, claim for their "factive"/"non-factive" contrast.
12. White, 1972.
13. E.g., Russell, 1918, 218.
14. Cp. MacIntosh, 1980.
15. E.g., Ayer, 1956, *passim,* esp., 12, 14, 18, 25, 28, 31, 35.
16. E.g., Ayer, 1956, 25, 150; Armstrong, D. M., 1973, 137–8, 198; Harman, 1973, 114.
17. Cp. Scheffler, 1956, 22.
18. Cp. Margolis, 1973, 4, 14, 24; Ackermann, 1972, 74; contrast Lehrer, 1974, 24–5.
19. *Categories* 7b25–30, *Metaphysics D,* § 15.
20. 88b–89b.
21. I. 3. 1.
22. § 4.
23. E.g., Ayer, 1936.
24. E.g., Ayer, 1936, *passim*
25. E.g., Hume, 1748. § 4.
26. Cp. Lewy, 1944; Malcolm, 1942; Ayer, 1936, 72, 91
27. E.g., thesis quoted by Malcolm 1950, 245.
28. E.g., Ayer, 1940. 45; 1936, 127; Hume, 1738, 1. 4, 1; Descartes, *Meditations* I.
29. E.g., *De Interpretatione,* 18b 11–15; cp. Taylor, 1957.
30. E.g., Ayer, 1936, Chs. 4–5; 1940, 43–5.
31. Cp. White, 1975, Chs. 1–3.
32. E.g., Locke, *Essay,* IV, *passim*
33. Rozeboom, 1967, esp. 288, accepts both theses.
34. Moore, 1959, 240; 1962, 277–9; cp. Rollins, 1967.
35. In Moore, 1959, he sometimes said that "It is certain that p" implies "I know that p," but in Moore, 1962, 277, he moved to the view that "It is certain that p" implies "*Somebody* knows that p." I argue that both views are wrong.
36. E.g., Moore, 1962, 184; 1959, 197, 205 *et passim*.
37. E.g., Moore, 1959, 235, 241; 1962, 277–9; cp. the philosophical barbarism "certain for (or to) somebody," e.g., Heidelberger, 1963, 243; Firth, 1967, 3–27.

38. Hacking, 1967.
39. As Moore sometimes did, e.g., 1959, 220, 222, 238–41.
40. E.g., Heidelberger, 1963, 243–4; cp. Robinson, 1971, 22.
41. Incidentally A. Naess's opinion poll method of doing philosophy showed that the vast majority of his subjects thought that "p" is indeed equivalent to "It is certain that p" as well as to "It is true that p."
42. E.g., Moore, 1962, 278; cp. 1959, 240–1.
43. E.g., Locke, *Essay,* IV. 3; Ayer, 1956.

CHAPTER FOUR

1. Cp. Danto, 1968, Lehrer, 1974, Ackermann, 1972, Armstrong, D. M., 1973, Ayer, 1956.
2. Cp. Sosa, 1970, 63; Danto, 1968, 73; Woozley, Ayer, Hospers, Chisholm, Urmson, Hintikka, (references given in Danto, 1968, 73, footnote); Scheffler, 1965, 21, 23; Rynin, 1967, 10.
3. E.g., Armstrong, D. M., 1973, 138.
4. Cp. Locke, *Essay,* Book IV, *passim;* Prichard, 1950, reprinted in Griffiths, 1967, 86.
5. Contrast Chisholm, 1957, 19.
6. Contrast Locke, *Essay,* IV. xi. 9; Moore, 1953, 273; 1959, 239; Malcolm, 1963, 59, 244; Ayer, 1956, Ch. I; Aaron, 1956, 1–13.
7. E.g., Wittgenstein, 1969, § 8; contrast § 308.
8. E.g., Moore, 1959, 227, 236, 239; 1953, 273; Malcolm, 1963, 25 and 32; contrast 229; Hintikka, 1962, 116–22; Chisholm, 1957, 19.
9. Contrast "He'll come for certain," which does mean "He'll certainly come," that is, "It is certain that he will come."
10. As Wittgenstein, 1969, § 15, seems to have thought.
11. E.g., Prichard, 1950, reprinted in Griffiths 1967, 85 ff., Ackermann, 1972, 68, 105–6; cp. Butchvarov, 1970, 89, who seems to argue the opposite on the ground that any justification for KKp is less certain than the justification of Kp (contrast. 28, where KKp is said to imply and be implied by Kp on the ground that the evidence for both is identical); Hintikka, 1962, Ch. 5, says "K virtually implies KK," but his "virtually implies" seems to be an attempt to eat one's cake and have it. Contrast, e.g., Rynin, 1967, 29–30; Danto, 1967, 121, 149–53; Lemmon, 1967. Plato, *Charmides* 167bff., raises the question.
12. Butchvarov, 1970, *passim,* though realising this difference, seems to assimilate them and the "unthinkability of being wrong that p," as contrasted with the "impossibility" of this, as all equivalent to knowing that p.
13. E.g., Lehrer, 1974, 55–63; cp. Woozley 1953, reprinted in Griffiths, 1967, 95; who seems to accept this for "knowing that," but not for "knowing what, where, etc."
14. Quoted by Hintikka, 1962, 108.
15. E.g., Cohen, 1962.
16. Woozley, 1953, reprinted in Griffiths, 1967, 94–6, alleges that "A knows that . . . ." implies, whereas "A knows *what* . . . ." does not, that A can show that his answer is right (Lehrer, 1974, 55 ff., also holds that "knows that . . . ,"—and possibly also "knows what"—implies knowing that one's answer is right). But if, as I have argued, e.g., "A knows what the size of x is" implies "A knows that the size of x is so and so," then Woozley's view would result in a contradiction.

17. Cp. Danto, 1967, 32–53.
18. E.g., Lehrer, 1974, 63–74.
19. Cp. Mannison, 1976, 553–4.
20. E.g., Cohen, 1962, Hintikka, 1962; Lehrer, 1974.
21. E.g., Lehrer, 1974; Radford, 1966.
22. E.g., Hamlyn, 1970, Ch. 4 (a); Lehrer, 1974, Ch. 3; Ackermann, 1972, Chs. 5
and 6; Soza, 1974; Swain, 1974; Butchvarov, 1970; 30–2; Scheffler, 1965, Ch. 5;
Armstrong, D. M., 1973, Ch. 10; Harman, 1973, 113–4; Harrison, 1963; Chisholm,
1957, 16; Hospers, 1956, 146–8; Rozeboom, 1967, 257–68, who says "its essentially
non-controversial," Plato, *Meno* and *Theaetetus*. Contrast Danto, 1968, 153–5.
23. E.g., Ring., 1977, 51–9.
24. E.g., Ayer, 1956; Lehrer, 1974; Danto, 1968; Woozley, 1948.
25. *Pace,* Armstrong, D. M., 1973, 143 fl.
26. E.g., Chisholm, 1957, 17–18.
27. E.g., Ayer, 1956, Ch. 1.
28. E.g., Chisholm, 1966; Meyers and Stern, 1973.
29. E.g., Malcolm, 1952; Scheffler, 1965, 8–9.
30. E.g., Hoffman, 1970, 150–4; Lehrer, 1974.
31. Cp. Ayer, 1956; Chisholm, 1966; Woozley, 1948; Harrison, 1963; Rozeboom,
1967; Arner, 1959; 84–92; Saunders, 1966.
32. Cp. Coder, 1974.
33. Cp. Gettier, 1963; Clark, 1964, 11; Skyrms, 1967; Sosa, 1974; Saunders,
1966; Harman, 1973.
34. Lehrer's denial, 1970, 125–6; 1974, 19–21; of this depends on supposing that
in his examples one's justification for believing that someone V's does not "pass
through" the false *premise* that X V's. But just as the probability of k on e, in his
example, "depends on" that of h on e and on the implication of k by h, so the
justification of believing that someone V's "depends on"—as he really admits in
1974, 2—the justification for falsely believing that X V's. We must distinguish the
illegitimate use of something false as a reason for Ving and the legitimate use of
justifiably believing something false as a reason for Ving.
35. *Theaetetus,* 208b.
36. Russell, 1912, Ch. 13.
37. E.g., Rozeboom, 1967; Pailthorp, 1969; Meyers and Stern, 1973; and a
somewhat weaker principle in Armstrong D. M., 1973, Ch. 14, § 1.
38. E.g., Thalberg, 1969; Pailthorp, 1969; Margolis, 1973; Lehrer, 1974, 216–7,
227; Meyers and Stern, 1973.
39. For references, see Swain, 1974, 15, footnote 3; cp. Olen, 1976.
40. As Unger, 1967, who critically denies empirical theories—contrast Harman,
1967.
41. Cp. Ayer, 1956; Lehrer, 1971; Harman, 1970; Swain, 1972; Sosa, 1974.
42. Cp. Harman, 1970.
43. Cp. Swain, 1972; Skyrms, 1967.
44. Cp. White, 1961.
45. E.g., Goldman, 1967; contrast Steiner, 1973.
46. E.g., Sosa, 1969.
47. Cp. Unger, 1967, 1968; cp. Grant, 1980; contrast Harman, 1967. Even those
who make justified belief a necessary part of the analysis of knowledge insist that
the belief must "not depend on any false statement," e.g., Lehrer, 1974, 21, note 9
and references cited.
48. Cp. the articles and bibliography in Pappas and Swain, 1978.

CHAPTER FIVE

1. *Meditations.*
2. Letter to Stillingfleet; *Essay,* II. 1. 4.
3. E.g., Ewing, 1951.
4. E.g., Scheffler, 1965, 28–31; who, despite criticisms of a different kind from mine of Ryle, accepts the thesis; cp. Adams, 1958, 300–06; who says that "know" is both a "capacity dispositional achievement verb" and an "episodic achievement verb." Barnes, W. H. F., 1956, 67–9, does distinguish for perceptual verbs, like "see," "hear," etc., an "achievement" use and a "state" or "experience" use, but not for "know." I think the distinction is implausible for perceptual verbs. Cp. Lemmon, 1967, 65; Landesman, 1970, 4; Evans, 1978, 41–2, 44, 137. Armstrong, D.M., 1973, 177–8; though not saddling Ryle with the "achievement" thesis, does himself subscribe to it in suggesting that "A knowing that something is the case is more usefully compared with the successful *manifestation* on a particular occasion of an ability to do something."
5. 1949, 149–53.
6. *Pace* Adams, 1958.
7. Ryle, 1954, 109.
8. Armstrong, D. M., 1973, slides from "know" to "come to know."
9. E.g., Prichard, 1950, reprinted in Phillip's 1967, 81–9; Armstrong, D. M., 1973, 189.
10. E.g., Malcolm, 1958, 87–92.
11. Contrast Prichard, 1950, 86–8.
12. E.g., Prichard, 1950, 88–9.
13. E.g., Aaron, 1956; contrast Woozley, 1953; White, 1957; 1972.
14. Austin, 1946, 169–75; contrast Harrison, 1962.
15. Contrast Beversluis, 1971.
16. *Philosophical Grammar* § 10, Basil Blackwell, Oxford, 1974.

Bibliography

[of references in the footnotes]

Aaron, R. I. 1956. "Feeling Sure," *Proceedings Aristotelian Society*, Suppl. 30, 1–13.

Ackermann, R. J. 1972. *Belief and Knowledge*, Doubleday, New York.

Adams, E. M. 1958. "On Knowing That," *Philosophical Quarterly*, 8, 300–6.

Armstrong, D. M. 1973. *Belief, Truth and Knowledge*, Cambridge U.P., London.

Armstrong, J. H. S. 1953. "Knowledge and Belief," *Analysis*, 13, 111–17.

Arner, D. 1959. "On Knowing," *Philosophical Review*, 68, 84–92.

Austin, J. L. 1946. "Other Minds," *Proceedings Aristotelian Society*, Suppl. 20, 148–87.

Ayer, A. J. 1936. *Language, Truth and Logic*, Gollancz, London.

———. 1940. *The Foundations of Empirical Knowledge*, Macmillan, London.

———. 1956. *The Problem of Knowledge*, Penguin, Harmondsworth, Middlesex.

Barnes, J. 1980. "Paradoxes in Plato's Distinction between Knowledge and True Belief," *Proceedings Aristotelian Society*, Suppl. 54, 193–206.

Barnes, W. H. F. 1956. "On Seeing and Hearing," in *Contemporary British Philosophy*, III, ed. H. D. Lewis, 65–81. Allen and Unwin, London.

Beversluis, J. 1971. " 'I Know': An Illocutionary Analysis," *Southern Journal of Philosophy*, 9, 345–52.

Braithwaite, R. B. 1933. "The Nature of Believing," *Proceedings Aristotelian Society*, 33, 129–46.

Brett, N. 1974. "Knowing How, What and That," *Canadian Journal of Philosophy*, 4, 293–300.

Brown, D. G. 1970. "Knowing How and Knowing That, What," in *Ryle*, ed. O. P. Wood and G. Pitcher, Doubleday, New York, 213–48.

———. 1974. "Reply to Brett," *Canadian Journal of Philosophy*, 4, 301–3.

Butchvarov, P. 1970. *The Concept of Knowledge*, Northwestern U. P., Evanston.

Carl, W. and Horstmann, R. P. 1972. "Knowing and Claiming," *Ratio*, 14, 155–171.

Carr, D. 1979. "The Logic of Knowing How and Ability", *Mind*, 88, 394–409.

Chisholm, R. M. 1957. *Perceiving*, Cornell U. P., Ithaca.

———. 1966. *Theory of Knowledge*, Prentice-Hall, Englewood Cliffs.

———. 1976. "Knowledge and Belief: De Dicto and De Re," *Philosophical Studies*, 29, 1–20.

Clark, M. 1964. "Knowledge and Grounds: A comment on Mr. Gettier's paper," *Analysis* 24, 46–8.

Coder, D. 1974. "Naturalising the Gettier Argument," *Philosophical Studies*, 26, 111–18.

Cohen, L. J. 1962. "Claims to Knowledge," *Proceedings Aristotelian Society*, Suppl. 36, 63–75.

Danto, A. C. 1967. "On Knowing That we Know," in *Epistemology: New Essays in the Theory of Knowledge*, ed. A. Stroll, Harper and Row, New York, 32–53.

———. 1968. *Analytical Philosophy of Knowledge*, Cambridge U. P., Cambridge.

Dunn, R. and Suter, G. 1977. "Zeno Vendler on the objects of Knowledge and
    Belief," *Canadian Journal of Philosophy*, 7, 103–14.
Evans, J. L. 1978. *Knowledge and Infallibility*, Macmillan, London.
Ewing, A. C. 1951. *Fundamental Questions of Philosophy*, Routledge and Kegan
    Paul, London.
Firth, R. 1967. "The Anatomy of Certainty", *Philosophical Review*, 76, 3–27.
Geach, P. T. 1977. *Providence and Evil*, Cambridge U. P., Cambridge.
Gettier, E. L. 1963. "Is justified true belief knowledge?", *Analysis*, 23, 121–3.
Goldman, A. 1967. "A Causal Theory of Knowing," *Journal of Philosophy*, 64,
    357–72.
Gould, J. 1955. *The Development of Plato's Ethics*, Cambridge U. P., Cambridge.
Grant, B. 1980. "Knowledge, Luck and Charity," *Mind*, 89, 161–81.
Griffiths, A. P. 1967. ed. *Knowledge and Belief*, Oxford U. P., London.
Hacking, I. 1967. "Possibility," *Philosophical Review*, 76, 143–68.
Hamlyn, D. W. 1970. *The Theory of Knowledge*, Macmillan, London.
Harman, G. H. 1967. "Unger on Knowledge," *Journal of Philosophy*, 64, 353–9.
———. 1970. "Knowledge, Reasons, and Causes," *Journal of Philosophy*, 67,
    841–55.
———. 1973. *Thought*, Princeton U. P., Princeton.
Harrison, J. 1962. "Knowing and Promising," *Mind*, 71, 443–57.
———. 1963. "Does Knowing Imply Believing," *Philosophical Quarterly*, 13,
    322–332.
Heidelberger, H. 1963. "Knowledge, Certainty and Probability," *Inquiry*, 6,
    242–50.
Hintikka, J. 1962. *Knowledge and Belief*, Cornell U. P., Ithaca.
Hoffman, R. 1970. *Language, Minds and Knowledge*, London.
Hospers, J. 1956. *An Introduction to Philosophical Analysis*, Routledge, London.
Jones, O. R. 1975. "Can One Believe What One Knows?," *Philosophical Review*,
    84, 220–35.
Kiparsky, P. and Kiparsky, C. 1971. "Fact" in *Semantics*, ed. Steinberg, D. D. and
    Jakobovits, L. A. Cambridge U. P., Cambridge, 345–69.
Klein, P. 1971. "A Proposed Definition of Propositional Knowledge" *Journal of
    Philosophy*, 68, 471–82.
Landesman, C. 1970. ed. *The Foundations of Knowledge*, Prentice-Hall, Engle-
    wood Cliffs.
Lehrer, K. 1970. "The Fourth Condition of Knowledge: A Defense" *Review of
    Metaphysics*, 24, 122–8.
———. 1971. "How Reasons give us Knowledge, or the Case of the Gypsy
    Lawyer," *Journal of Philosophy*, 68, 311–13.
———. 1974. *Knowledge*, Oxford U. P., London.
Lemmon, E. J. 1967. "If I Know, do I Know that I Know?" in *Epistemology*, ed. A.
    Stroll, Harper and Row, New York, 54–82.
Lewy, C. 1944. "On the Relation of some Empirical Propositions to their Evi-
    dence", *Mind*, 53, 289–313.
Malcolm, N. 1942. "Certainty and Empirical Statements," *Mind*, 51, 18–46.
———. 1950. "The Verification Argument" in *Philosophical Analysis*. ed. M.
    Black, Cornell U. P. Ithaca.
———. 1952. "Knowledge and Belief," *Mind*, 61, 178–89.
———. 1954. "On Knowledge and Belief," *Analysis* 14, 94–8.
———. 1958. Wittgenstein: *A Memoir*, Oxford University Press, London.

———. 1976. "Moore and Wittgenstein on the Sense of 'I Know'," *Acta Philosophica Fennica*, 28, 216–40.

MacIntosh, J. J. 1980. "Knowledge and Belief", *Proceedings Aristotelian Society*, 80, 169–85.

Mannison, D. 1976. "Why Margolis hasn't defeated the Entailment thesis," *Canadian Journal of Philosophy* 6, 553–9.

Margolis, J. 1973. *Knowledge and Existence*, Oxford University Press, London.

Mayo, B. 1964. "Belief and Constraint," *Proceedings Aristotelian Society*, 64, 139–56.

Meyers, R. G. and Stein, K. 1973. "Knowledge without Paradox," *Journal of Philosophy*, 70, 147–60.

Moore, G. E. 1953. *Some Main Problems of Philosophy*, Allen and Unwin, London.

———. 1959. *Philosophical Papers*, Allen and Unwin, London.

———. 1962. *Commonplace Book*, Allen and Unwin, London.

Munsat, S. 1966. *The Concept of Memory*, Random House, New York.

Olen, J. 1976. "Is Undefeated Justified True Belief Knowledge?", *Analysis*, 36, 150–2.

Pailthorp, C. 1969. "Knowledge as Undefeated Justified True Belief," *Review of Metaphysics*, 22, 25–47.

Pappas, G. S. and Swain, W. 1978. eds. *Essays on Knowledge and Justification*, Cornell, U. P., Ithaca.

Price, H. H. 1935. "Some Considerations about Belief," *Proceedings Aristotelian Society*, 35, 229–52.

Prichard, H. A. 1950. "Knowing and Believing," in *Knowledge and Perception*, Oxford U. P., London.

Prior, A. N. 1971. *Objects of Thought*, Oxford University Press, London.

Pollock, J. L. 1974. *Knowledge and Justification*, Princeton U. P., Princeton.

Radford, C. 1966. "Knowledge—by example," *Analysis*, 27, 1–11.

Ring, M. 1977. "Knowledge—The Cessation of Belief," *American Philosophical Quarterly*, 14, 51–60.

Robinson, R. 1971. "The Concept of Knowledge," *Mind*, 80, 17–28.

Rollins, C. D. 1967. "Certainty" in *Encyclopaedia of Philosophy*, ed. P. Edwards, Collier-Macmillan, New York, II, 67–71.

Rozeboom, W. W. 1967. "Why I know so much more than you do" *American Philosophical Quarterly*, 4, 257–68.

Russell, B. A. W. 1912. *The Problems of Philosophy*, Oxford U. P., London.

———. 1918. "The Philosophy of Logical Atomism," reprinted in *Logic and Knowledge*, ed. R. C. Marsh, Allen and Unwin, London (1956).

———. 1940. *An Enquiry into Meaning and Truth*, Allen and Unwin, London—pagination from Penguin, ed., Harmondsworth, 1962.

Ryle, G. 1946. "Knowing how and Knowing that," *Proceedings Aristotelian Society*, 46, 1–16.

———. 1949. *The Concept of Mind*, Hutchinson, London.

———. 1954. *Dilemmas*, Cambridge U. P., Cambridge.

Ryner, D. 1967. "Knowledge, Sensation and Certainty," in *Epistemology*. ed. A. Stroll, Harper and Row, New York, 8–31.

Saunders, J. T. 1966. "Does Knowledge require Grounds?," *Philosophical Studies*, 17, 7–13.

Scheffler, I. 1965. *Conditions of Knowledge*, Scott, Foreman, Chicago.

Skyrms, B. 1967. "The Explication of 'X knows that p'," *Journal of Philosophy*, 64, 373–89.

Snell, B. 1924. "Die Ausdrücke für den Begriff des Wissens in der Vorplatonischen Philosophie," *Philologische Untersuchungen*.

Sosa, E. 1970. "Two Conceptions of Knowledge," *Journal of Philosophy*, 67, 59–66.

———. 1974. "The Concept of Knowledge: How do you know?," *American Philosophical Quarterly*, 11, 113–22.

Steiner, M. 1973. "Platonism and the Causal Theory of Knowledge," *Journal of Philosophy*, 70, 57–66.

Swain, M. 1972. "Knowledge, Causality and Justification," *Journal of Philosophy*, 69, 291–360.

———. 1974. "Epistemic Defeasibility," *American Philosophical Quarterly*, 11, 15–25.

Taylor, R. 1957. "The Problem of Future Contingencies," *Philosophical Review*, 66, 1–28.

Thalberg, I. 1969. "In Defense of Justified True Belief," *Journal of Philosophy*, 66, 794–803.

Unger, P. 1967. "Experience and Factual Knowledge," *Journal of Philosophy*, 64, 152–73.

———. 1968. "An Analysis of Factual Knowledge," *Journal of Philosophy*, 65, 157–170.

Vendler, Z. 1972. *Res Cogitans*, Cornell U. P., Ithaca.

———. 1978. "Escaping from the Cave: A Reply to Dunn and Suter," *Canadian Journal of Philosophy*, 8, 79–87.

Warnock, G. J. 1962. "Claims to Knowledge," *Proceedings Aristotelian Society*, Suppl. 36, 51–63.

White, A. R. 1957. "On Claiming to Know," *Philosophical Review*, 66, 180–92.

———. 1961. "The Causal Theory of Perception," *Proceedings Aristotelian Society*, Suppl. 35, 153–68.

———. 1972. "What we Believe," *American Philosophical Quarterly*, Monograph 6, 69–84.

———. 1974a "Review of *Res Cogitans*," *Mind*, 83, 466–8.

———. 1974b "Can What is Known and What is Believed be the Same?," *Hermathena*, 118, 139–46.

———. 1975. *Modal Thinking*, Blackwell, Oxford.

Wittgenstein, L. 1969. *On Certainty*, Basil Blackwell, Oxford.

Wolgast, E. H. 1978. *Paradoxes of Knowledge*, Cornell U. P., Ithaca.

Woozley, A. D. 1949. *Theory of Knowledge*, Hutchinson, London

———. 1953. "Knowing and not Knowing," *Proceedings Aristotelian Society*, 53, 151–72.

Wright, H. von. 1963. *Norm and Action*, Routledge and Kegan Paul, London.

Index

(not including names mentioned only in the reference and bibliography)